ORGANIZATIONAL AUTHORITY

The Atherton Press Political Science Series

*Published simultaneously in Great Britain
by Prentice-Hall, International, London*

ORGANIZATIONAL AUTHORITY

Superior-Subordinate Relationships
in Three Public Service Organizations

Robert L. Peabody

ATHERTON PRESS

A Division of Prentice-Hall, Inc.

70 Fifth Avenue, New York 10011

1964

ORGANIZATIONAL AUTHORITY
Superior-Subordinate Relationships
in Three Public Service Organizations

Robert L. Peabody

Preface

The purpose of this book is to present the results of an exploratory study of authority relationships in three public service organizations. The three organizations—an elementary school, a public welfare agency branch office, and a municipal police department—were selected to provide moderate to complex hierarchical structures and variation in the degree to which *functional* authority as distinct from *formal* authority might be emphasized. By functional authority I mean authority based on technical knowledge and personal skills— in other words, competence and influence. By formal authority I mean authority based on legitimacy, position, and the rewards and sanctions inherent in position. This is the more conventional mean- ing of authority, a phenomenon which has often been defined in the literature of the social sciences as legitimate, sanctioned, or institu- tional power. As the results of this study suggest, both types of authority are necessary for achieving goals and satisfying individual needs through organizational activity, but the appropriate combi- nations and the effectiveness with which they are exercised remain matters requiring further empirical inquiry.

v

In organizations of any complexity, authority relations are basic to the achievement of organizational goals. Yet, conflicting attitudes toward authority would also seem to be a major source of tension and anxiety in organizations. In the short run, the perceptions of authority reported here may result in a better understanding of authority relations on the part of both superiors and subordinates. In the long run, more systematic research may lead to more precise use of such concepts as authority and to an empirically based theory of organizational behavior.

My obligations to other students of organizations have been recorded in part in the footnotes of this study. My intellectual indebtedness to Max Weber, Chester I. Barnard, Herbert A. Simon, and Peter M. Blau needs particular emphasis. Here I wish to acknowledge a more immediate and special indebtedness to three members of my doctoral dissertation committee at Stanford University. Prof. Robert A. Walker was particularly helpful in formulating the problem and keeping my attention focused on its central dimensions. Prof. Heinz Eulau contributed immeasurably to the theoretical and empirical aspects of the study. Prof. Edmund H. Volkart provided me with a sounding board for ideas and offered insightful comments which were most helpful during the early draft stages. I am also obligated to a number of readers of parts of earlier versions of the manuscript, in particular, the encouragement and comments of Alex Bavelas, Robert K. Bierstedt, Milton C. Cummings, Jr., William J. Gore, Jan Hajda, M. Kent Jennings, Herbert Kaufman, F. P. Kilpatrick, Hubert Marshall, James A. Robinson, Arthur L. Stinchcombe, Donald W. Taylor, James D. Thompson, and Dwight Waldo. I owe a special debt, as well, to Cornelius P. Cotter for editorial advice and assistance. Of course, I alone am responsible for any errors of fact or interpretation.

This study could not have been accomplished without the cooperation of the members of the three public agencies which provided the field setting. Regrettably, these persons must remain unnamed in order to preserve their anonymity as well as that of their organizations. However, I would like to express my appreciation to the top executives who gave me permission to observe their organizations as well as those administrators and workers who participated in the formal interviews. These people not only made this inquiry much easier than I had anticipated it would be, but also impressed me with their capabilities as public servants and with their cordiality as individuals.

Part of Chapter II and Chapter IV first appeared as "Authority Relations in Three Organizations," *Public Administration Review,* XXIII (June 1963), 87–92. Chapter VII first appeared as "Perceptions of Organizational Authority: A Comparative Analysis," *Administrative Science Quarterly,* VI (March 1962), 463–482. I am grateful to the editors and publishers for permission to use this material here, somewhat modified, to make an integrated book.

This study was financed in part by a grant from the Stanford University Committee on Research in Public Affairs. A Brookings Institution Research Fellowship for 1960–1961 and financial assistance from The Johns Hopkins University Committee on Research in Public Affairs greatly aided revision.

The typists—Mrs. Nadine Cline, Mrs. Doris Stude, and Mrs. Mary Gill—deserve special commendation for their first-rate work.

Finally, I must acknowledge the encouragement, support, and sense of humor of my wife, Judy, to whom this book is appreciatively dedicated.

Robert L. Peabody

Baltimore
1964

Contents

ix

Contents

List of Tables and Figures

I

Conceptions of Authority:
The Problem

All of us are familiar with authority. Yet, the question "What is authority?" is so broad as to be almost unanswerable. One way to begin is to distinguish between authority as a phenomenon, as a word used in everyday language, and as a more-or-less precise, technical concept.

The phenomenon of authority is all around us. Parent-child, teacher-pupil, expert-layman, employer-employee, master-servant, ruler-ruled—all of these relationships imply authority. Any thorough inquiry into the types of authority, the conditions facilitating its acceptance, and the functions it performs at different levels of society and among different cultures would be almost as encompassing as the study of human interactions themselves.

The word "authority" has a wide and varied meaning in everyday language. The preacher relies on the authority of the scriptures. Writers refer to the authority of the dictionary for the correct spelling of words. Frequently the word is used as a synonym for expertness: Clarence Cannon is an authority on parliamentary procedure; Charles Goren, an authority on bridge; Werner von Braun, an authority on rocket technology and guided missiles. A golf professional may instruct the beginner to "hit the ball with authority." The newspapers urge creation of a Golden Gate authority, a particular type of government institution. Workers complain about the arbitrary authority of the boss when he shortens the coffee break. Authority is a multipurpose word—a word conveying a number of meanings in many different contexts.

The use of authority as a technical concept is not much more precise, despite its extended use in theology, philosophy, and the social sciences. Authority has been a central concept in the discussions of man's relationship to an ultimate authority, God, and in debates over the relative spheres of church and state. Since the beginning of political society, man has speculated about the nature and justification of political authority. As Bertram de Jouvenel has observed:

> The phenomenon called "authority" is at once more ancient and more fundamental than the phenomenon called "state"; the natural ascendancy of some men over others is the principle of all human organizations and all human advances.[1]

Closely akin to these political and philosophical treatments of authority has been the body of literature which defines authority as a special kind of power or influence, such as "formal power" or "legitimate influence." The thesis advanced in this chapter is that authority is at least analytically distinct from such related phenomena as power and influence on the one hand and leadership on the other. The first issue is particularly complex and clouded, namely, how authority compares with and differs from such seemingly related forms of human interaction as power and influence. There seems to be more general agreement among social scientists concerning a second issue, that is, the need for analytical distinction between authority relations and leader-follower relations or leadership. Although every student of authority must come to grips with these issues if only to make distinctions which serve his immediate

---

[1] *Sovereignty* (Chicago: University of Chicago Press, 1957), p. xiii.

purposes, claims at definitive resolution would seem to be premature, if not naïve. For explicative purposes, authority can be analytically distinguished, in any given organizational setting, from power, influence, or leadership, but it is inextricably fused with these related phenomena. The fact that authority relations are never found in pure form is not a valid objection to attempts at developing more precise analytical distinctions nor does it alleviate the need to work toward operational definitions of these concepts. The student of authority should be aware of the magnitude of the problem, for these concepts are unavoidably abstract, segmented, and exaggerated notions of an elusive reality.

Before elaborating on these analytical distinctions, several additional limitations on the focus of this study should be made explicit. A number of field settings exist for the exploration of authority by social scientists: the family (parental authority); small groups (informal authority and influence); intermediate organizations beyond face-to-face groups, including bureaucracies (organizational and bureaucratic authority); and relations between the citizen and his government and the state (political authority). The boundaries between these various kinds of authority are not clear-cut; they often interact in important ways. The primary focus of this study, however, will be organizational authority, particularly authority in bureaucratic organizations.

Psychologists, biologists, and physiologists have long been aware that biological systems, including human beings, differ greatly in their response to different drugs, environments, and social stresses. Obviously, the personal characteristics of individuals may also be expected to influence their readiness to accept the authority of others. Much of the work on authoritarianism can be interpreted as dealing with this problem. Fascinating as this aspect of the problem of authority is, it, too, must be relegated to the periphery. Such analysis would require depth interviews, personality tests, and individual case histories. The primary focus here is on social relations rather than individual human differences which may predispose one person to accept, another to reject, authority.

Finally, numerous studies bridging the gap between the findings of one discipline and those of other disciplines are needed. To what extent do authority patterns developed in infancy and childhood carry over into adult relations in bureaucratic organizations? Two prominent students of organizational behavior would seem to take exactly opposite views on this complex matter. Thus, Chris Argyris asserts that "the individual does not tend to react to others (e.g., the boss) in terms of patterns learned during childhood," whereas Robert Presthus maintains that "from infancy on the individual is trained to defer to authority. He develops over time a generalized deference to the authority of parenthood, experience, knowledge, power and status." Elsewhere Presthus asserts: "It seems equally clear that personality structures are not discarded like snakes' skins when one enters the bureaucratic arena; rather the patterns of bureaucratic authority and deference reflect the values of institutions through which the bureaucrat has grown, primarily the family." No attempt at reconciliation of the divergent viewpoints of Argyris and Presthus will be attempted here. Both await further empirical investigation.[2]

Conversely, what impact do so-called democratic and totalitarian cultural norms have on the exercise of authority in the subsystems making up society? Reinhard Bendix's comparative analysis of the ideologies of management in four countries at different times— Russia under the tsars, England in the early stages of industrialization, America at the time of the scientific-management and human-relations movements, and East Germany after World War II— suggests the kind of research which is needed to resolve problems of this kind.[3]

Important and intriguing as some of these questions and settings are, they must remain outside the scope of this work. The boundaries of the present study are delineated in greater detail in the following sections, which set forth more elaborate statements

[2] The quote by Argyris is from his article, "The Individual and Organization: An Empirical Test," *Administrative Science Quarterly*, IV (1959), 145–167. The quotes from Presthus are taken from two articles: "Toward a Theory of Organizational Behavior," *Administrative Science Quarterly*, III (1958), 48–72, 57; and "Behavior and Bureaucracy in Many Cultures," *Public Administration Review*, XIX (1959), 25–35, 27.

[3] *Work and Authority in Industry* (New York: John Wiley & Sons, 1956).

of distinctions between authority and related terms, the problem of organizational authority, and the research setting of this study.

AUTHORITY, POWER, AND INFLUENCE

The exacting task of differentiating authority from such related phenomena as power and influence has a long and honorable history in the literature of the social sciences.[4] In general, social scientists have adopted one of three approaches: (1) they have used these terms interchangeably with no explicit distinctions between them; (2) they have defined authority as a special case of power or influence; or (3) they have treated authority, power, and influence as different kinds of relationships between people or groups, with each kind of relationship worthy of research in its own right. Most definitions of authority in the literature of the social sciences fall within the second classification, that is, definitions which adopt the genus-and-differentia approach and view authority as a special case of power or influence.[5] For example, authority has been defined as

[4] Among the major works on power, authority, and influence written by twentieth-century social scientists and philosophers, the following are representative but obviously not exhaustive: Edward Banfield, *Political Influence* (New York: Free Press of Glencoe, 1961); Dorwin Cartwright, ed., *Studies in Social Power* (Ann Arbor: Institute for Social Research, University of Michigan, 1959); Robert A. Dahl, *Who Governs?* (New Haven: Yale University Press, 1961); Carl J. Friedrich, ed., *Authority* (Cambridge: Harvard University Press, 1958); Harold D. Lasswell, *Politics: Who Gets What, When, How* (New York: Meridian Books, 1958); Harold D. Lasswell and Abraham Kaplan, *Power and Society* (New Haven: Yale University Press, 1950); Charles E. Merriam, *Political Power* (New York: McGraw-Hill, 1934); Richard E. Neustadt, *Presidential Power* (New York: John Wiley & Sons, 1960); C. Wright Mills, *The Power Elite* (New York: Oxford University Press, 1959); Bertrand Russell, *Power* (New York: W. W. Norton, 1938); Bertrand Russell, *Authority and the Individual* (Boston: Beacon Press, 1960); Max Weber, *From Max Weber: Essays in Sociology*, ed. H. H. Gerth and C. Wright Mills (New York: Oxford University Press, 1958); and Max Weber, *The Theory of Social and Economic Organization*, ed. A. M. Henderson and Talcott Parsons (New York: Oxford University Press, 1947).

[5] Carl G. Hempel, "Fundamentals of Concept Formation in Empirical Science," *International Encyclopedia of Unified Science* (Chicago: University of Chicago Press, 1952), II, No. 7, 5–6; Morris R. Cohen and Ernest Nagel, *An Introduction to Logic and Scientific Method* (New York: Harcourt, Brace & Co., 1934), p. 235.

"the power to make decisions which guide the actions of another," "formal power," "institutionalized power," "legitimate influence," "legitimate power," and "socially sanctioned power."[6] Such definitions may provide some leads for differentiating authority from power and influence; however, until social scientists are able to formulate more precise operational definitions of power and influence per se, the practice of defining authority as a special case of these already elusive concepts would seem of limited value.

The third approach which is prevalent in the literature treats authority as a phenomenon worthy of investigation on its own merit. Without denying that for many purposes analytical distinctions between such terms as power, influence, authority, and control may be useful, this approach focuses on authority as a basic kind of action occurring between people or groups. A number of theoretical contributions have set the stage for the present study of organizational authority. Among the most important of these are Max Weber's classification of the types of authority according to the kind of claim to legitimacy typically made by each; Chester Barnard's formulation of the implications of subjective authority; and the subsequent development of these treatments of organizational authority by a number of American social scientists, most notably Herbert Simon and Peter Blau. These and other contributions will be examined at some length in the next chapter.

AUTHORITY AND LEADERSHIP

In contrast to the general ambiguity and elusiveness of definitions of authority vis-à-vis power and influence, there seems to be considerable agreement in the literature of social science that authority relations (headship, domination, or formal office) should be clearly distinguished from leader-follower relationships (informal

---

[6] Herbert A. Simon, *Administrative Behavior* (2d ed.; New York: Macmillan Co., 1957), p. 125; Lasswell and Kaplan, *op. cit.,* p. 133; Robert K. Bierstedt, "An Analysis of Social Power," *American Sociological Review,* XV (1950), 736; Bernard Barber, *Social Stratification* (New York: Harcourt, Brace & Co., 1957), p. 236; Amitai Etzioni, *A Comparative Analysis of Complex Organizations* (New York: Free Press of Glencoe, 1961), p. 14; Richard A. Schermerhorn, *Society and Power* (New York: Random House, 1961), p. 5.

leadership or personal influence). To put this point another way, although power, influence, and leadership occur between, within, and without formal or institutionalized organizational structures, it is generally conceded that authority is confined to relations between people occupying hierarchical positions in formal organizations. Leadership is more comprehensive than authority; it may or may not be engaged in by those who formally occupy so-called positions of authority. L. F. Urwick, a long-time student of administration, has put this point succinctly:

> There are, in every organization, those who exercise leadership, that is to say, to whom others go for advice and whose influence, deliberately or unconsciously, guides their actions, who have no place in the official structure of the organization at all.[7]

A second fundamental distinction frequently made between authority and leadership is in respect to their base or source. Under this conception the major sources of authority are considered to be impersonal and derived from above; leadership, in contrast, is spontaneously accorded to the leader by his fellow group members as a result of certain personal qualities possessed by the leader. A number of social scientists have made similar distinctions between informal leadership and bureaucratic authority, for example, Cecil Gibb, Peter Blau, and Robert Bierstedt.[8] A quotation from Bierstedt is illustrative:

> But leadership is not authority. . . . Leadership depends upon the personal qualities of the leader in the situation in which he leads. In the case of authority, however, the relationship ceases to be personal and, if the legitimacy of the authority is recognized, the subordinate must obey the command even when he is unacquainted with the person who issues it.

---

[7] *Leadership in the Twentieth Century* (New York: Pitman Publishing Corp., 1957), p. 37.

[8] Cecil A. Gibb, "Leadership," in Gardner Lindzey, ed., *Handbook of Social Psychology* (Reading, Mass.: Addison-Wesley, 1954), II, 882; Peter M. Blau, *The Dynamics of Bureaucracy* (Chicago: University of Chicago Press, 1955), p. 178; Robert K. Bierstedt, "The Problem of Authority," in Morroe Berger, Theodore Abel, and C. H. Page, eds., *Freedom and Control in Modern Society* (New York: Van Nostrand & Co., 1954), pp. 71–72.

> In a leadership relation the person is basic; in an authority
> relation the person is merely a symbol.[9]

One note of caution should be made explicit, however. As was
suggested earlier, in any given organizational setting, authority and
leadership are frequently fused. When a strong leader occupies a
position of authority, the probabilities of achieving organizational
goals and satisfying individual needs are both increased. However,
ultimate acceptance of authority, as with leadership, rests with subordinates or followers, thus qualifying the notion that authority is
delegated down the organizational hierarchy. In any event, the idea
of leadership as a personal quality may be usefully distinguished
from the idea of leadership as an organizational function.

> The first refers to a special combination of personal char-
> acteristics; the second refers to the distribution throughout an
> organization of decision-making powers. The first leads us
> to look at the qualities and abilities of individuals; the second
> leads us to look at the patterns of power and authority in
> organizations. Both of these ideas or definitions are useful,
> but it is important to know which one is being talked about,
> and to know under what conditions the two must be consid-
> ered together in order to understand a specific organizational
> situation.[10]

Why one more attempt at clarification of this concept when
most people have an intuitive grasp of its meaning and so many
definitions and interpretations already exist in the literature? If
organizational theory is to develop, social scientists must move beyond the crude intuitive understanding of such phenomena as power,
influence, leadership, and authority, toward relatively precise and
necessarily abstract concepts, both as a means of understanding and
explanation and, it is hoped, prediction. Although numerous definitions of authority exist in the literature of administration, management, and organizational behavior, a review of these writings reveals
considerable contrast, vagueness, and ambiguity in the use of the

---

[9] *Loc. cit.*
[10] Alex Bavelas, "Leadership: Man and Function," *Administrative Science Quarterly,* IV (1960), 491.

concept. As Chapter II will demonstrate, many of these definitions are open to criticism for their one-sided emphasis. They frequently fuse description, evaluation, and prescription. Finally, relatively few of these treatments of authority combine theoretical analysis with systematic empirical inquiry. The most obvious grouping in a large organization is that composed of the superior and his immediate subordinates, but, unless one includes the multitude of studies devoted to leadership styles, there are relatively few systematic explorations of this basic relationship.

THE RESEARCH PROBLEM AND ITS SETTING

The focus of this study may be simply stated: Why do some people (subordinates) obey other people (superiors) in organizations? Yet, as has been already noted, this simple statement leads to a number of complex problems. How is authority distinguished from the use of force and coercion, on the one hand, and the use of persuasion and personal influence, on the other hand? Is authority directly observable, and, if not, what indicators will attest to the fact that authority is being exercised? It seems reasonable to assume that superiors and subordinates view authority differently, but along what dimensions and to what extent? What are the implications of differential perception for (1) the achievement of organizational goals and (2) the attainment of individual satisfactions?[11]

A number of leading students of management and administration have emphasized the importance of authority in organizations. Luther Gulick, co-editor of the influential *Papers on the Science of Administration,* describes the problem of organization as one of creating an authority structure which will ensure an effective network of communication and control between the executive at the

---

[11] Chester I. Barnard, *The Functions of the Executive* (Cambridge: Harvard University Press, 1938), pp. 55–59. The importance of these two criteria—what Barnard terms "effectiveness" (the achievement of organizational goals) and "efficiency" (the satisfaction of individual needs) —is continually restated in the literature of organizational theory. See, for example, Mason Haire's discussion of "productive efficiency" in Mason Haire, ed., *Modern Organizational Theory* (New York: John Wiley & Sons, 1959), p. 4.

center and the subdivisions of work on the periphery.[12] Chester I. Barnard, in one of the first systematic attempts to set forth a theory of organization, stresses the importance of authority not only in facilitating communication and control, but in securing essential services from organizational contributors.[13] Herbert A. Simon, the author of another management classic, identifies three contributions of authority to administration organizations: the enforcement of responsibility, the specialization of decision-making, and the co-ordination of activity.[14] Writing in 1958, Harold J. Leavitt, a small-group psychologist, discusses authority as a basic technique of managerial control and coordination.[15] Almost endless examples of a similar nature can be culled from the literature of administration and the social sciences. To a lesser extent these students have also pointed up the conflict-producing and tension-invoking implications of authority. Discipline and control may inhibit initiative and crea-tivity on the part of subordinates. They may hesitate to assume or go out of their way to avoid responsibility. Communication from subordinates to superiors may be stifled precisely because the former is subordinate to the latter. A worker may tell his boss only what he thinks his boss wants to hear. Despite these potential inhibiting and disruptive consequences, authority remains an inevitable aspect of complex organizations. Indeed, the complexity often reflects the number of levels of hierarchy and diverse units of an organization. It is important, therefore, to make explicit several additional as-sumptions about the research setting of this study before turning to a more intensive analysis of these problems through a review of the treatment of the concept of authority in the literature of administration.

The focus is on internal authority relations in small to medium-sized bureaucratic organizations. Three public service organizations

[12] Luther Gulick, "Notes on the Theory of Organization," in Luther Gulick and Lyndall F. Urwick, eds., *Papers on the Science of Administration* (New York: Institute of Public Administration, 1937), p. 7.

[13] Barnard, *op. cit.,* chap. xii.

[14] Simon, *op. cit.,* chap. vii.

[15] *Managerial Psychology* (Chicago: University of Chicago Press, 1958), chap. xi.

—a suburban elementary school, a county public welfare branch office, and a municipal police department—constitute the field setting. The study is further limited to one culture and one time—the American culture in the mid-twentieth century. Some of the implications of these limitations require elaboration. To begin with, what is meant by the terms "organization" and "bureaucracy"?

Dwight Waldo succinctly states the two horns of a dilemma which confronts any investigator when he attempts to define a phenomenon like organization.

> On the one hand it seems cavalier, even outrageously slipshod, to try to proceed to a careful examination of any phenomena without an attempt to define, that is, to understand and agree upon, what the object of examination is, at least in general terms and as now understood. On the other hand, one can argue persuasively that the scientific enterprise has no close and necessary relationship to conventional definitions, that the verbal difficulties outweigh the scientific gain, that the problem of definition can really only be solved by by-passing it and proceeding to activities that eventually will "define" in meaningful, operational terms.[16]

A partial way out of this dilemma is to adopt the strategy employed by March and Simon—to give examples of what is meant by organization rather than to define the term.[17] Thus, each of the agencies providing the field setting for this study is clearly an organization. Each, in turn, is part of a larger and more complex organization—the Forest Heights School District, the Orchard County Welfare Department, and the government of Garden City.[18] All of these organizations are part of the local government organization of Western State, which, along with other state governments and countless private industrial organizations, associations, and primary groups, can, in turn, be subsumed under a supra-organization, the United States of America. One thing that all of these organizations

[16] Dwight Waldo, "Organizational Theory: An Elephantine Problem," *Public Administration Review*, XXI (1961), 223.

[17] James G. March and Herbert A. Simon, *Organizations* (New York: John Wiley & Sons, 1958), p. 1.

[18] All proper names here are pseudonyms, used to protect the anonymity of these organizations and their personnel.

have in common is goals. They all fall within Barnard's definition of formal organization as "a system of consciously coordinated activities of two or more persons."[19]

Of course, the more complex the organization, the more difficult it is to identify specific goals and reconcile conflict between goals which may be at cross-purposes. How should a fire department divide its resources—time, man power, equipment—between preventing fires and putting them out once they start? What is the ultimate goal of the Strategic Air Command? Is it to prevent a nuclear strike by an enemy or to provide an effective counterstrike should such an attack be launched? If one goal has clear priority over another, it, too, will require a different allocation of resources. The goals of a nation-state are even more difficult to identify and reconcile. The preamble to the Constitution of the United States can be considered an initial attempt. But generations of statesmen and constitutional lawyers can testify to the difficulty, for example, of reconciling the quest for "a more perfect union" with the securing of "the blessings of liberty."

Once an organization begins to pursue several goals simultaneously and, particularly, increases in size, it inevitably assumes bureaucratic tendencies. Although bureaucracy is a term of ambiguous meaning, it is used here in its neutral and nonderogatory sense to convey the notion of a certain kind of formal organization, one that is administrative, task-oriented, and complex. Following the classic analysis of Weber, certain basic characteristics of bureaucratic organizations may be specified. Blau suggests four characteristics: specialization, a hierarchy of authority, a system of rules, and impersonality.[20] Although the present study concentrates primarily on the second, some of the implications of the other characteristics will be developed in subsequent chapters.

---

[19] *Op. cit.,* p. 73. "As a formal analytical point of reference, *primacy of orientation to the attainment of a specific goal* is used as the defining characteristic of an organization which distinguishes it from other types of social systems." Talcott Parsons, "Suggestions for a Sociological Approach to the Theory of Organizations," *Administrative Science Quarterly,* I (1956), 64.

[20] *Bureaucracy in Modern Society* (New York: Random House, 1956), pp. 17–19.

Bureaucratic characteristics are obviously not confined to the public sphere. Although the three organizations selected for the field phase of this study are public organizations, a similar study could have been conducted in industrial organizations. Governmental and private bureaucracies have much in common, but one should not minimize important differences. "Above all else, government is differentiated from other activities by its public nature, which represents both its exposure to public scrutiny and its concern with the public interest."[21] Government employees are constantly confronted with a complex dependency relationship which consists of both a responsibility to and an authority over individual citizens. This relationship is particularly acute in police departments, but it has its counterpart in the relationship of welfare workers to recipients and schoolteachers to parents and children. But generalizations about the effect of this peculiar kind of ambivalent relationship on the internal dynamics of organizational authority are impossible to arrive at without more empirical research. A number of additional questions of importance to the exercise of authority within governmental organizations can only be posed, not answered. Does public employment attract a particular kind of person, one who is both more dedicated to service and more interested in job security? It is often suggested that civil-service provisions make it more difficult to remove incompetent employees than do the terms of private employment, but no comparative studies are available. How important is seniority for promotion in government as compared with private industry? In the absence of further studies, perhaps the only safe observation is that generalizations from this study to the private sphere should be made with even more caution than those to other governmental organizations.

Generalizations from this study are further qualified by the relatively small size of the three organizations studied: a welfare branch office with twenty-three members, a police department with thirty-three members, and an elementary school with twenty-one members. However, each organization is also a subdivision of a medium-sized bureaucracy: the county government, city government,

<hr>

[21] Marver H. Bernstein, *The Job of the Federal Executive* (Washington, D.C.: Brookings Institution, 1958), p. 201.

and school district. Both the parent organizations and the sub-divisions actually studied were large enough to necessitate a formal authority structure. However, these suborganizations were small enough so that all members knew one another. Another consequence of their size was that day-to-day operations were considerably affected by the activities of internal cliques. These points are elaborated in Chapter IV.

Scientific generalizations about authority relationships in organizations would seem to depend on (1) the development and refinement of concepts which will guide observation and analysis of data and (2) the evolution of research methods and techniques which will relate concepts to empirical observations. In the last analysis, generalizations about authority relationships must be exposed to and confirmed by concrete, observable events, hence the need for developing empirical indicators of acceptance of authority and for formulating working hypotheses which can be subjected to empirical inquiry. This study reports on perceptions of authority in three public organizations. No claims are made as to the representativeness of these organizations. The interview data are suggestive rather than conclusive proof of the hypotheses. This, then, is an exploratory study aimed at clarifying the concept of organizational authority and establishing certain guidelines for further investigation.

II

Organizational Authority:
A Review of the Literature

A number of uses of the concept of authority in the literature of the social sciences were illustrated in Chapter I by references to different field settings for the study of authority, including bureaucratic organizations. Before setting forth the research design used in this study, some of the major treatments of the concept of authority in the literature of administration, management, organization, and bureaucracy need to be sketched. Innumerable definitions and interpretations of authority prevail in this literature. They reflect different disciplines within the social sciences, different approaches by academicians and practitioners, and even somewhat contradictory formulations by the same student of authority at various times. No attempt at a detailed or exhaustive chronicle of these definitions will be presented, even if it were possible for one student of organization theory to trace and grasp them. Rather, the object will be to outline several major approaches to the definition and interpretation of authority in organizations. These approaches, for want of better names, may be labeled (1) the conventional or formal approach,

15

(2) the human-relations or informal approach, and (3) reconciling or converging approaches, the last category including theoretical analyses as well as selected empirical inquiries.[1]

Logically, classification of definitions under these three broad rubrics should begin by specifying certain criteria which these definitions must meet before they are classified. Ideally, each set of criteria would determine a certain class, and the classes thus determined would be mutually exclusive and jointly exhaustive.[2] In part because of the complexity of the empirical phenomenon, in part because of inherent ambiguities in our everyday language, and in part because earlier definitions were not without their impact on later formulations, these conditions of exclusiveness and exhaustiveness cannot be met. Instead, definitions of authority may be located along a series of continua which seem to be characteristic of these major approaches:

The Conventional Approach	Converging Approaches	The Human-Relations Approach
Property or attribute	————————————	Relationship
Formal	————————————	Informal
Rational	————————————	Nonrational
Impersonal	————————————	Subjective
Control from the top	————————————	Acceptance by the subordinate

[1] This chapter benefits considerably from more broadly oriented surveys of the literature of administration, management, and organization in the following works: Dwight Waldo, *The Administrative State* (New York: Ronald Press, 1948); Bendix, *op. cit.;* Chris Argyris, *Personality and Organization* (New York: Harper & Bros., 1957); and March and Simon, *op. cit.* While this chapter was in draft form, a closely parallel review of the literature of leadership theories was published by Warren G. Bennis en-

The property-relationship continuum comes closest to meeting the requirements of formal classification. Most definitions of authority fit readily into one or the other class. On the one hand, authority is viewed as an attribute of an office, for example, "authority is the capacity to issue orders." On the other hand, authority is viewed as a relationship between two persons, one superior and one subordinate. The other continua suggested above are seldom so clearcut. That is to say, these distinctions are formulated in terms of polarities rather than dichotomies. Thus, differing conceptions of authority are more-or-less formal, impersonal, and so on.

Generally speaking, those who view authority as a property inherent in office have tended to emphasize the formal, rational, impersonal, and control-from-the-top aspects of authority and organization. This will be referred to as "the conventional approach." Conversely, those who conceptualize authority as a relationship have tended to emphasize the informal, nonrational, subjective, and acceptance-by-the-subordinate aspects of authority and organizational behavior. This view of authority will be labeled "the human-relations approach." Within the past twenty-five years, there has been a definite synthesizing and reconciliation of these contrasting definitions of the concept so as to incorporate all these aspects into the interpretation of authority. Several of the more prominent of these attempts will be reviewed under "converging approaches."

The earliest definitions in the literature with which this analysis will be concerned tend to emphasize the conventional and formal aspects of authority. During the 1920's and 1930's, even as this conventional analysis was at its height, revised definitions of authority stressing the informal and human-relations aspects began

titled "Leadership Theory and Administrative Behavior: The Problem of Authority," *Administrative Science Quarterly*, IV (1959), 259–301. See also Douglas McGregor's contrast between "theory X, the traditional view of direction and control," and "theory Y," an attempt to modify the traditional view based on accumulated human-relations research, *The Human Side of Enterprise* (New York: McGraw-Hill, 1960); and Terence K. Hopkins, "Bureaucratic Authority: The Convergence of Weber and Barnard," in Amitai Etzioni, ed., *Complex Organizations* (New York: Holt, Rinehart & Winston, 1961), pp. 82–98.

2 Hempel, *op. cit.*, p. 51.

to appear. Since the late 1930's, but particularly after World War
II, definitions of authority combining both approaches have been
prevalent. Although most of the authors under review have written
of authority as one of several concepts or a system of concepts, it is
impossible to comprehensively appraise these systems and their con-
sistency or congruency. At the most, this brief survey hopes to bring
some order to the terminology of management and administration
by identifying some common elements and accounting for some of
the differences in these definitions. At the least, this review will pose
some of the complex semantic problems confronting the student
of authority as he attempts to abstract the more penetrating insights
from a half-century of commentary, characterized for the most part
by vagueness and ambiguity. This chapter, then, consists of an
abbreviated chronological development of definitions of authority
in the literature of management and organization. Particular emphasis has been placed on a review of the literature of public
administration.

THE CONVENTIONAL APPROACH:
ORGANIZATIONS WITHOUT PEOPLE

As has been suggested, the conventional approach to authority
emphasized the formal, rational, impersonal, control-from-the-top
aspects of authority. Authority was most characteristically defined
as an attribute of office as distinct from a relationship between the
incumbents of formal positions. This approach emphasized the ra-
tionality and predictability of organizational activity and, for the
most part, tended to ignore the motivations and attitudes of the
human beings who were employed by the organization. Max Weber's
theoretical treatment of bureaucracy, Frederick W. Taylor's scientific-management movement, and the administrative-management
theory associated with Luther Gulick and L. F. Urwick typify this
conventional approach to authority.

Max Weber and Bureaucratic Authority

Weber's theoretical contributions to the study of bureaucracy
and his classification of three basic types of authority are so well

known as to need no comprehensive review here.[3] His treatment of bureaucracy, of which authority based on office or position is a basic characteristic, provides the framework for most contemporary analysis of bureaucratic behavior by American sociologists. Weber makes use of the distinction between authority based on office and authority based on personal attributes to differentiate the first of his three pure types of authority—legal-rational authority—from his second and third types—traditional and charismatic authority.

> In the case of legal authority, obedience is owed to the legally established impersonal order. It extends to the persons exercising the authority of office under it only by virtue of the formal legality of their commands and only within the scope of authority of the office. In the case of traditional authority, obedience is owed to the *person* of the chief who occupies the traditionally sanctioned position of authority and who is (within its sphere) bound by tradition. But here the obligation of obedience is not based on the impersonal order, but is a matter of personal loyalty within the area of accustomed obligations. In the case of charismatic authority, it is the charismatically qualified leader as such who is obeyed by virtue of personal trust in him and his revelation, his heroism or his exemplary qualities so far as they fall within the scope of the individual's belief in his charisma.[4]

Weber's treatment of legal-rational authority distinguishes between, but does not elaborate on, authority inherent in office and authority based on technical knowledge and expertise. With regard to the former, "the typical person in authority occupies an 'office.' . . . The members of the corporate group, in so far as they obey a person in authority, do not owe this obedience to him as an individual, but to the impersonal order."[5] Furthermore, for Weber bureaucratic authority is ". . . the most rational known means of carrying out

[3] For extended commentary on Weber's typology of authority, see Talcott Parsons' introduction to *Theory* . . . , *op. cit.*, pp. 56–77; Reinhard Bendix, *Max Weber: An Intellectual Portrait* (Garden City, N.Y: Doubleday & Co., 1960), pp. 289–449, especially 294–300; and Peter M. Blau, "Critical Remarks on Weber's Theory of Authority," *American Political Science Review,* LVII (1963), 305–316.

[4] Weber, *Theory* . . . , *op. cit.*, p. 328.

[5] *Ibid.*, p. 330.

imperative control over human beings. It is superior to any other form in precision, in stability, in the stringency of its discipline, and in its reliability."[6]

Weber's interpretation must, of course, be evaluated in terms of the historical perspective and cultural settings of which he wrote. As an ideal construct it should be distinguished from the more descriptive school of British and American administrative theorists.

Luther Gulick: The Structure of Authority

Another body of literature with much the same emphasis as Weber's formal interpretation is the traditional administrative-management literature of the first third of the twentieth century. Beginning with the scientific-management movement launched by Frederick Taylor, the orientation of this body of writers received its classic expression in the *Papers on the Science of Administration*, published in 1937. Taylor formulates no explicit definition of authority. He and his early followers concentrate primarily on the basic physical activities involved in production processes rather than on interactions between management and workers. Although the major objectives of the scientific-management movement seem to coincide with those of most employers, for Taylor the science of work performance is designed to eliminate friction between employers and workers. The techniques of scientific management, themselves, are to be the ultimate authority.[7]

Luther Gulick's treatment of authority in his famous paper, "Notes on the Theory of Organization," may be taken as characteristic of the approach of the classical organization theorists.[8] It is in this noted essay that Gulick sets forth the famous POSDCORB as a mnemonic device for recalling executive functions in administration.

Although Gulick never explicitly defines authority, he seems

---

[6] *Ibid.*, p. 337.

[7] Frederick W. Taylor, *The Principles of Scientific Management* (New York: Harper, 1911), and *Scientific Management* (New York: Harper & Bros., 1947). For extended commentaries on Taylor and the scientific-management movement, see Waldo, *The Administrative State, op. cit.*, pp. 47–61; and Bendix, *Work and Authority . . .* , *op. cit.*, pp. 247–287, esp. p. 281.

[8] Gulick and Urwick, *op. cit.*, pp. 1–45.

to use the term in at least three ways. Most predominantly, authority is equated with the network of hierarchical positions in the organization—"the structure of authority" or "the system of authority." He also uses the word with reference to the top executive or directive board. "It is clear from long experience in human affairs that . . . a structure of authority requires not only many men at work in many places at selected times, but also a single directing executive authority."[9] Finally, authority is used as a synonym for expertness based on superior knowledge. He warns against the assumption of expertness in one field on the basis of specialized competence in another. "Another trait of the expert is his tendency to assume knowledge and authority in fields in which he has no competence. . . . They do not remember that the robes of authority of one kingdom confer no sovereignty in another. . . ."[10]

Although Gulick recognizes that the problem of organization must be approached from both top and bottom, the major thrust is still in terms of effective control:

> . . . Those who work from the top down must guard themselves from the danger of sacrificing the effectiveness of the individual services in the zeal to achieve a model structure at the top, while those who start from the bottom, must guard themselves from the danger of thwarting co-ordination in their eagerness to develop effective individual services.[11]

The emphasis is placed on executive leadership in the achievement of organizational goals. Not only is coordination achieved by organization; it is also achieved through ideas. "Accordingly, the most difficult task of the chief executive is not command, it is leadership, that is, the development of the desire and will to work together for a purpose in the minds of those who are associated in any activity."[12]

As late as 1943, despite the impact of the human-relations movement, a writer intimately associated with Gulick and the traditional administrative-management theorists, Lyndall Urwick, still defines authority as "the right to require action of others." How-

[9] *Ibid.*, p. 7.
[10] *Ibid.*, pp. 10–11.
[11] *Ibid.*, p. 11.
[12] *Ibid.*, p. 37.

ever, in language predictive of later analyses by Simon, Presthus, and others, Urwick goes on to suggest that authority "may be (a) formal, i.e., conferred by the organization; (b) technical, i.e., implicit in special knowledge or skill; or (c) personal, i.e., conferred by seniority or popularity."[13]

In sum, then, ideas of authority—of having authority, of exercising authority, of delegating authority—are constantly met in the traditional literature of administration and management. Throughout this literature, as with Weber's theoretical analysis of bureaucracy, emphasis is placed on the formal, impersonal aspects of authority. As Bierstedt restates the case for the formal interpretation of authority: "In the ideal case the exercise of authority is wholly objective, impartial, impersonal, and disinterested."[14] People are relegated to square boxes in organization charts. Management manipulates the workers in "the one best way" in order to achieve its predetermined goals. The "supreme coordinating authority" originates at the top of the structural hierarchy and flows down the "chain of command." Following Weber's interpretation, concepts of authority often assume autocratic overtones. Military organization is put forth as the model. One of the best examples of this aspect of the traditional definition of authority is found in the following excerpt from a standard public-administration textbook published in 1950:

> Lines of authority lead up through this administrative hierarchy; authority passes down from the top, through successive levels of management, to the first-line supervisor, while information and reports pass up through the same channels from the first-line supervisor to the top. In a military organization authority passes down from the general, through the lieutenant generals and major generals, the colonels, majors, captains, and lieutenants, to the noncommissioned officers—the lowest level in the line of authority. A comparable situation exists in civilian organizations; the names are different but the principle is the same.[15]

[13] Lyndall F. Urwick, *The Elements of Administration* (New York: Harper & Bros., 1944), p. 42.

[14] Berger, Abel, and Page, *op. cit.,* p. 76.

[15] W. Brooke Graves, *Public Administration in a Democratic Society* (Boston: D. C. Heath & Co., 1950), pp. 40–41.

Even as this conventional view of authority reached its peak of acceptance in the literature of management and administration in the 1930's, a countertrend—the human-relations approach to authority, calling attention to the importance of informal organization and nonrational aspects of organizational behavior—was under way.

THE HUMAN-RELATIONS APPROACH: PEOPLE WITHOUT ORGANIZATIONS

The human-relations movement, in part an extension of the scientific-management movement and in part a continuation of the management-oriented literature of pre–World War II, drastically altered, if it did not reverse, many of the implications of the older organization theory. In the tradition of the scientific managers, the human-relations specialists hoped to discover laws of human behavior in organizations, but laws which took into account nonrational and emotional factors. The literature of human-relations research has been extensively appraised and reviewed. The concern here is much narrower, namely, to examine its approach to the concept of authority. In contrast with the conventional treatment, this new approach defined authority in relational terms, stressing its informal, nonrational, and subjective aspects. The hierarchy of authority was virtually turned upside down. Innumerable writers contributed to this movement, but two of its founders, Mary Parker Follett and Elton Mayo, will be taken as representative of the human-relations movement in their treatment of authority.

Mary Parker Follett and "The Illusion of Final Authority"

Mary Parker Follett, a lecturer and writer on subjects ranging from democratic theory to management practices, was one of the first people to call for a science of human relations.[16] In *Creative*

---

[16] Among her numerous writings, *The New State* (New York: Longmans, Green & Co., 1920) and *Creative Experience* (New York: Longmans, Green & Co., 1924) were probably her two major works. A collection of her administrative essays has been assembled in *Dynamic Administration,* ed. Henry C. Metcalf and Lyndall Urwick (New York: Harper & Bros., 1942). The title of this section is taken from her article of the same name,

Experience she chastises the social sciences for not utilizing recent developments of thought, including behavioral psychology and Gestalt principles:

> . . . They are not all of them even using the most modern *method* of study, which is wholly to abandon the region of abstract speculation and to study the behavior of men. . . . The greatest need of today is a keen, analytical objective study of human relations.[17]

This remarkable woman was also, perhaps, the first to challenge the traditional notions of authority in administration. The notion of an ultimate authority at the apex of the hierarchy is an illusion. "Instead . . . of supreme control, ultimate authority, we might perhaps think of cumulative control, cumulative authority." Decision-making takes place at all levels of the hierarchy, not just at the top. "An executive decision is a moment in a process. The growth of a decision, the accumulation of authority, not the final step, is what we need most to study."[18] Authority was viewed as a shared and cooperative activity.

> The form of organization should be such as to allow or induce the continuous coordination of the experiences of men. Legitimate authority flows from coordination, not coordination from authority.[19]

In the final analysis, the study of authority and of organizational behavior in general, are psychological issues. Miss Follett's papers on management and administration are replete with such concepts as "constructive conflict," "the psychology of consent and participation," "coordination," and "integration." Perhaps her major contribution, as far as the analysis of authority is concerned, is the

---

originally appearing in the *Bulletin of the Taylor Society*, XI (1926), 243–246. This article is reprinted in part in Albert Lepawsky, ed., *Administration* (New York: Alfred A. Knopf, 1955), pp. 326–327.

[17] *Op. cit.,* p. ix.
[18] Lepawsky, *op. cit.,* pp. 326–327.
[19] *Ibid.,* p. 327.

attention she focuses on the psychological conditions which make for spontaneous and effective consent.

Elton Mayo and "The Inducement of Spontaneous Cooperation"

The American Management Association had begun to focus attention on the human factors in the industrial setting as early as the 1920's, but the human-relations movement was formally launched with the work of Elton Mayo and his Harvard Business School associates in their classic studies at the Hawthorne Plant of the Western Electric Company.[20] Although Mayo shares Taylor's belief in science as the foundation on which an enlightened management should base its approach to the workers, his emphasis is on the attitudes and emotions of the workers rather than the basic physical activities involved in production. The Hawthorne experiments began with a study of lighting in relation to worker output; they culminated in a broad inquiry into worker morale and job satisfaction. No attempt will be made here to review these and other research findings relating to informal organization, communication, and morale. Our primary focus must be limited to Mayo's reinterpretation of the meaning of managerial authority in industry.[21]

In *The Social Problems of an Industrial Civilization,* Mayo reports three conclusions resulting from his work and that of his associates. First, he calls attention to the importance of well-knit human groups or teams in industry: "Men's desire to be continuously associated in work with his fellows is a strong, if not the strongest, human characteristic." Second, rather than depend on tests of technical capacity, he urges management to concentrate on

[20] Elton Mayo, *The Social Problems of an Industrial Civilization* (Boston: Graduate School of Business Administration, Harvard University, 1945) and *The Human Problems of an Industrial Civilization* (Boston: Graduate School of Business Administration, Harvard University, 1946); F. J. Roethlisberger, *Management and Morale* (Cambridge: Harvard University Press, 1941); F. J. Roethlisberger and W. J. Dickson, *Management and the Worker* (Cambridge: Harvard University Press, 1938); T. W. Whitehead, *The Industrial Worker* (Cambridge: Harvard University Press, 1938).

[21] The following interpretation relies heavily on Bendix's analysis of the contributions of Elton Mayo to American managerial ideology. *Work and Authority . . . , op. cit.,* pp. 308–319.

developing the worker's social skills and general adaptability. Third, the task of management is seen as the encouragement of "the eager human desire for cooperative activity."[22] For Mayo:

> The administrator of the future must be able to understand the human-social facts for what they actually are, unfettered by his own emotion or prejudice. He cannot achieve this ability except by careful training—a training that must include knowledge of relevant technical skills, of the systematic ordering of operations, and of the organization of cooperation.[23]

In sum, management's task is to elicit willing cooperation. Worker satisfaction gained from allegiance to his own group and the larger organization is as important as material benefits. Acceptance of authority is generated by "spontaneous cooperation."[24]

This brief review of the human-relations approach to authority, as illustrated in the writings of Mary Parker Follett and Elton Mayo, does not do justice to the many ramifications of this approach. It does, however, convey the shift in emphasis from authority viewed as formal, rational, and impersonal control to an awareness of the importance of informal, nonrational, and subjective factors which condition acceptance of authority in organizations. This last point receives particular attention in the treatment of the "subjective aspect of authority" by Chester I. Barnard.

CONVERGING THEORETICAL APPROACHES

The beginning of modern organization theory may be dated from the publication of Barnard's classic, *The Functions of the Executive,* in 1938, although attempts to reconcile the conventional and human-relations approaches to authority have been predominantly a post–World War II phenomenon. Since 1945 an imposing and disparate cluster of theoretical analysis and empirical inquiries has been undertaken. For want of a better term, these may be grouped under the heading of "organizational behavior." Some

---

[22] *The Social Problems* . . . , *op. cit.,* pp. 111–112.

[23] *Ibid.,* p. 122.

[24] As Bendix notes, "The meaning of this term in the writings of Mayo and others is suggestive but obscure." It seems to imply a willing compliance which does not preclude the intrusion of managerial inducements. *Work and Authority* . . . , *op. cit.,* p. 318, n. 147.

students of administration seek to revise "the naive, unsubstantiated, and unrealistic aspects of the human relations approach without sacrificing its radical departure from traditional theory."[25] Others build on Weber's theoretical analysis of bureaucracy and early Anglo-American administrative theory through the incorporation of relevant sociopsychological dimensions. Others not only abandon these approaches, but take different views of what the problem is.[26] A number of studies combining theoretical analysis with empirical inquiry will follow an outline of two of the major theoretical analyses of authority, those developed by Chester I. Barnard and Herbert A. Simon. Research which seems to bear most directly on the present exploratory study will receive more extended comment.

Barnard and the Subjective Aspect of Authority

Information about the way people behave in organizations has been assembled from a wide range of sources, not the least of which have been summaries of personal experiences by executives and administrators. Unlike many practitioners who confine their writing on administrative behavior to biographical or anecdotal sketches, Chester I. Barnard, the president of the New Jersey Bell Telephone Company, undertook a systematic treatment of organization theory.[27] The concept of authority is central to his analysis of executive functions. In Barnard's terms:

> Authority is the character of a communication (order) in a formal organization by virtue of which it is accepted by a contributor to or "member" of the organization as governing the action he contributes; that is, as governing or determining what he does or is not to do so far as the organization is concerned.[28]

[25] For a review of three of these "revisionists"—Robert McMurry, Chris Argyris and Douglas McGregor—see Bennis, *op. cit.*, p. 273.

[26] For reviews of the diverse approaches characterizing organization theory and empirical research, see March and Simon, *op. cit.*; Argyris, *Personality . . .*, *op. cit.*; Haire, *op. cit.*; Peter M. Blau and Richard W. Scott, *Formal Organizations* (San Francisco: Chandler, 1962); and Etzioni, *A Comparative Analysis . . .*, *op. cit.*

[27] The conceptual scheme underlying *The Functions of the Executive* is set forth in Barnard's *Organization and Management* (Cambridge: Harvard University Press, 1948), chap. v.

[28] *Functions . . .*, *op. cit.*, p. 163.

Perhaps the most imaginative aspect of Barnard's definition of authority is his emphasis on the subjective aspect of authority—the subordinate's personal acceptance of the communication as authoritative. This interpretation of authority by Barnard, like an earlier discussion of "The Illusion of Final Authority" by Mary Parker Follett, reverses the traditional emphasis on authority as orders issued from above and promulgated down the "chain of command." Why do subordinates accept orders? In Barnard's view a person can and will accept authority when four conditions prevail: (1) when he understands the communication, (2) believes it to be consistent with organizational purposes *and* (3) in his own personal interests, and (4) is mentally and physically able to comply with the communication.[29] One reason that organizations continue despite their potentially chaotic base is the existence of a "zone of indifference" in each individual within which orders are acceptable without conscious questioning of their authority. This zone will be wide or narrow depending on the degree to which the rewards of membership in the organization exceed the burdens and sacrifices demanded. This zone of indifference reflects the individual's loyalty to or identification with the organization.[30]

Barnard's treatment of objective authority—the character of the communication which induces acceptance—is more conventional in its orientation. In the final analysis, the acceptance of authority depends on the cooperative personal attitude of both superiors and subordinates and an effective system of communication in the organization.[31]

Barnard's interpretation of authority has influenced a number of students of organization, including Peter M. Blau, George C. Homans, Robert K. Merton, Waino Suojanen, Robert Tannenbaum, and, most notably, Herbert A. Simon.[32]

[29] *Ibid.*, p. 165.
[30] *Ibid.*, p. 169.
[31] *Ibid.*, pp. 173–175.
[32] Simon, *Administrative Behavior, op. cit.*, chap. vii; *Models of Man* (New York: John Wiley & Sons, 1957), chaps, iv, xi; "Authority," in Conrad M. Arensberg *et al.*, eds., *Research in Industrial Human Relations* (New York: Harper & Bros., 1957), chap. vii; with Donald W. Smithburg

Simon: Motivations for the Acceptance of Authority

In the influential work, *Administrative Behavior,* first published in 1947, Herbert Simon's purpose was the construction of adequate linguistic and conceptual tools as a basis for scientific analysis of organizational behavior.[33]

> The first task of administrative theory is to develop a set of concepts that will permit the description, in terms relevant to theory, of administrative situations. These concepts, to be scientifically useful, must be operational; that is, their meanings must correspond to empirically observable facts or situations. The definition of "authority" . . . is an example of an operational definition.[34]

Simon's contribution, then, is to be measured in part by the extent to which he has developed a "scientifically useful" definition of authority. Although Simon asserts that he employs a definition "substantially equivalent to that put forth by C. I. Barnard,"[35] his interpretation fluctuates between adoption of Barnard's subjective aspect of authority and a return to the more conventional approach of Urwick and other earlier administrative theorists.

Simon's first and most frequently repeated definition of authority takes the following form:

> A subordinate is said to accept authority whenever he permits his behavior to be guided by the decision of a superior, without independently examining the merits of that decision.[36]

In Chapter VII, "The Role of Authority," however, he reverts to a definition in which authority is attributed to a "superior," although in the very next sentence its relational aspects are emphasized.

> "Authority" may be defined as the power to make deci-

---

and Victor A. Thompson, *Public Administration* (New York: Alfred A. Knopf, 1950), chaps. viii-ix; and with March, *op. cit.,* pp. 90–91.

[33] *Op. cit.,* p. xlv.

[34] *Ibid.,* p. 37.

[35] *Ibid.,* p. 11.

[36] *Ibid.,* pp. 11, 22. ". . . Authority has been defined in this study not in terms of the sanctions of the superior, but in terms of the behaviors of the subordinate." *Ibid.,* p. 130.

sions which guide the actions of another. It is a relationship
between two individuals, one "superior," the other "subordinate."[37]

According to Simon's conception, then, authority may be examined from several perspectives: (1) in terms of the subordinate's
subjective reaction and subsequent behavior, (2) in terms of the
superior as to whether in fact he makes decisions which guide the
actions of others, and (3) in terms of the relationship between the
two people who are involved. There is nothing wrong with examining and analyzing authority from a number of different perspectives; in fact, it is essential to our understanding of the phenomenon.
However, these contrasting interpretations should be explicitly recog-
nized as such. Thus, it makes a considerable difference whether a
subordinate anticipates orders and carries them out willingly, carries them out passively without questioning them, or obeys the
superior begrudgingly because of the threat of sanctions. If the
superior is forced to rely on the sanctions inherent in his position
and his authority is continually being tested, he is then on his way
to losing his authority. In Barnard's terms, the subordinate's "zone
of indifference" has been considerably reduced. He is likely to evade
or reject the next order. He may even be considering resignation.

At one point Simon seems to argue that authority should be
restricted to those instances in which the subordinate does not independently examine the merits of the decision; at other times he
recognizes that subordinates may accept authority even though consciously questioning the instructions. His definition of authority is
incomplete to the extent that it fails to account for the degrees of
acceptance.[38] Moreover, his definitions of authority are neither
"operational" nor defined in "purely objective and behavioristic
terms." His statement with regard to operational definition quoted
earlier needs further qualification on two counts: (1) his explana-

---

[37] *Ibid.,* p. 125.

[38] The implications of this distinction are elaborated in Chapter III
and Chapter VI of the present study. For an unsympathetic but insightful
critique of Simon's approach in general and his concept of authority in
particular, see Herbert J. Storing, "The Science of Administration: Herbert
A. Simon," in Herbert J. Storing, ed., *Essays on the Scientific Study of
Politics* (New York: Holt, Rinehart & Winston, 1962), pp. 63–150.

tion of the term "operational" is ambiguous, and (2) not all concepts need to be "operational" in order to be scientifically useful.

Simon does not describe the operations which are to be performed in order to determine whether authority has been accepted. Direct observation can reveal a great deal. There are any number of specific indicators of the presence of authority relationships: occupancy of formal position, deference paid to superiors, the predominant direction in which orders flow, and so on. Gestures may regulate behavior even more effectively than written orders or spoken commands. A raised eyebrow may bring about the same results as a verbal reprimand. But the crux of authority turns on the matter of acceptance. As Edward C. Banfield has noted in his critique of Simon's definition, it is almost impossible to define authority in purely objective behavioral terms:

> If one merely observes the behavior, including the verbal behavior, of two persons, one cannot tell whether they are in what Simon calls a relationship of authority. One cannot find out if A is accepting the premises of B without getting knowledge of the subjective states of both A and B.[39]

Survey research techniques provide a partial solution. It is possible to ask superiors and subordinates how they perceive authority and under what conditions they will accept or reject it. But such questions are at least two steps removed from actual behavior itself. These techniques assume that the respondents will accurately relate their perceptions and that people will, in the main, react the way they say they will.

The second point—that not all concepts need to be "operational" in order to be scientifically useful—was in much greater dispute among philosophers of science in 1947 than it is today. Simon, influenced by such logical positivists as P. W. Bridgman, Rudolf Carnap, and A. J. Ayer, adopted the narrower thesis of empiricism —that all concepts should be transformed into observables. A more liberal thesis of empiricism is widely accepted currently. As Hempel

---

[39] "The Decision-Making Schema," *Public Administration Review,* XVII (1957), 278–285, 282. For Simon's rebuttal, see " 'The Decision-Making Schema': A Reply," *Public Administration Review,* XVIII (1958), 60–63.

concludes after an extended discussion of these points: "insistence that every scientific concept be *defined* in 'operational' terms is unduly restrictive; . . . it would disqualify, among others, the most powerful theoretical constructs."[40] In any event, organization theory has not reached the stage of development at which it can be described as a system of general propositions and definitions or at which the concept of authority can qualify as one of these highly abstract constructs which need not be related to observables. A more appropriate strategy, given the present stage of development of organization theory, is to attempt to provide these concepts with as much empirical import as possible.

In subsequent elaborations of the concept of authority, Simon has been content with more modest objectives. His conception of authority "is a definition, not an empirical statement about behavior."[41] Among Simon's major contributions to the discussion of authority is his identification of four of the motivational bases underlying acceptance of authority: confidence (technical skills), social approval (identification), sanctions and rewards, and legitimation. Some empirical findings with regard to several of these bases are reported at length in Chapter VII. Simon's definition of authority has been widely disseminated and adopted.[42]

Among other theories of organizational behavior using authority as a central concept in diverse ways, those of Edward H. Litchfield, Talcott Parsons, and Robert V. Presthus should be noted.[43]

[40] Hempel, *op. cit.*, pp. 39–50, 41.

[41] Arensberg *et al.*, *op. cit.*, pp. 103–118, 103. See also Simon's discussion of authority in his introduction to the second edition of *Administrative Behavior*, *op. cit.*, pp. xviii, xxxiv-xxxv.

[42] See, for example, Robert Dubin, ed., *Human Relations in Administration* (Englewood Cliffs, N.J.: Prentice-Hall, Inc., 1951), pp. 188–195; Leonard C. White, *Introduction to the Study of Public Administration* (4th ed.; New York: Macmillan Co., 1955), p. 35; Leavitt, *op. cit.*, chap. xi; Cartwright, *op. cit.*, chap. vii; Daniel J. Duffy, "Authority Considered from an Operational Point of View," *Journal of the Academy of Management,* II (1959), 167–175; and Bernard H. Baum, *Decentralization of Authority in a Bureaucracy* (Englewood Cliffs, N.J.: Prentice-Hall, Inc., 1961), pp. 25–26.

[43] Edward H. Litchfield, "Notes on a General Theory of Administration," *Administrative Science Quarterly,* I (1956), 3–29; Talcott Parsons, "Suggestions for a Sociological Approach to the Theory of Organizations,"

EMPIRICAL STUDIES OF
ORGANIZATIONAL AUTHORITY

Although all organizations of any complexity or permanence require an authority structure or network of hierarchical positions, the form that authority relations take may vary greatly from organization to organization.[44] Among important factors affecting the exercise of authority and the type of authority structure, one could single out the purpose of the organization, its state of technological complexity, its size, its developmental stage, its recruitment process, and the extent of participation allowed its members in the making of critical decisions. Along a continuum defining participation would be, at one extreme, the temporary groups combined to achieve a single purpose—for example, several wives getting together to buy a wedding present for a mutual friend. At the other extreme would be such institutions as prisons and mental hospitals where some "members" (prisoners, patients) are almost completely subjected to the decisions of the staff. Other organizations fall somewhere in between. Thus, most voluntary organizations allow more participation in key decisions among rank-and-file members than do military organizations. Authority is more diffuse in professional organizations than in most industrial firms and governmental agencies. Such a continuum, along which the three organizations providing the field setting for this study can also be ranged, may be used as a way of ordering selected empirical inquiries of authority relations in various field settings (see Fig. 1). Beginning, then, with several studies of authority relations in small work groups and voluntary organizations, other studies will be reviewed under the following broad categories: educational, medical, and research institutions; industrial

---

Administrative Science Quarterly, I (1956), 64–85, 225–239; and Robert V. Presthus, "Toward a Theory . . . ," and "Authority in Organizations," *Public Administration Review*, XX (1960), 86–91. For a critique of Presthus's treatment of the concept of authority, see Robert T. Golembiewski, "Some Notes on Presthus' 'Authority in Organizations,' " *Public Administration Review*, XXI (1961), 171–175.

[44] James D. Thompson and Frederick L. Bates, "Technology, Organization, and Administration," *Administrative Science Quarterly*, II (1957), 325–343.

organizations; governmental agencies; military organizations; and
mental institutions and prisons.

Small Work Groups and Voluntary Associations

No attempt will be made here to review the findings of research on small groups in general or even its application to the
study of administrative behavior. Although not directly focusing on
authority relations, articles by Whyte, Sayles, and Golembiewski
point up the importance of informal work groups and command
groups for large organizations.[45] As Whyte and Sayles suggest, small
friendship cliques and command groups composed of a superior and
his immediate subordinates are two of the most basic kinds of small
groups in any bureaucracy. Golembiewski's review of research on
small groups and its implications for public administration is directly relevant to this study. For example, he points out that sharp
differences in formal and informal rankings are a major cause of
group friction, which may, in turn, lead to low productivity. Promotional patterns which do not take into account informal leadership are apt to lead to the undermining of formal authority.

Studies of authority patterns in voluntary associations are rare.
Harrison examines modes for legitimizing authority in the relatively
autonomous local units of the American Baptist Convention and
concludes that Weber's typology is inadequate for the analysis of
voluntary associations. These organizations, by definition, place high
value on individual freedom to join, participate, and resign from
the association. He develops three subcategories of Weber's typology: rational pragmatic, quasi-charismatic, and mimetic-tradi-
tional.[46] Results of a study by Tannenbaum in over one hundred
geographically separate local Leagues of Women Voters suggested
that both leaders and members in effective leagues exercised more

---

[45] William F. Whyte, "Small Groups in Large Organizations," in John
Rohrer and Muzafer Sherif, eds., *Social Psychology at the Crossroads* (New
York: Harper & Bros., 1951); Leonard R. Sayles, "Work Group Behavior
and the Larger Organization," in Arensberg *et al., op. cit.*, pp. 131–145;
Robert T. Golembiewski, "The Small Group and Public Administration,"
Public Administration Review, XIX (1959), 149–156, 150.

[46] Paul M. Harrison, "Weber's Categories of Authority and Voluntary
Associations," *American Sociological Review*, XXV (1960), 232–237.

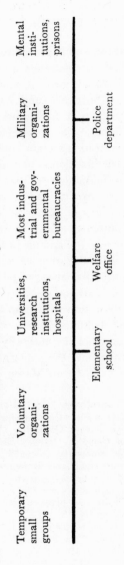

Fig. 1

Authority Continuum Showing the
Estimated Placement of Subject Organizations

control than did those in less effective leagues. Thus, a greater total of control was ascribed to the effective leagues.[47]

Educational, Medical, and Research Institutions

Other relatively unresearched areas for the study of authority relations are educational, medical, and research institutions. In his article, "Authority Structure and Organizational Effectiveness," Amitai Etzioni suggests a framework for such studies.[48] Etzioni maintains that three major generalizations from the traditional literature of administration are not applicable to professional organizations. These generalizations—that professional authority should be subordinate to line authority, that organizations are headed by "managers" and not "experts," and that organizations have one and only one ultimate center of authority (unity of command)—are not characteristic of authority as it is exercised in research institutions, universities, and psychiatric and medical clinics.[49]

Educational administration as a field of study is undergoing radical change. James has analyzed professional authority in educational settings, and Clark has discussed the strengths and limitations of faculty authority in university administration.[50] These theoretical analyses have been bolstered by a number of empirical studies, including Becker's study of the authority of the teacher in the metropolitan public school and the extensive examination of the school superintendent's role by Gross, Mason, and McEachern.[51]

---

[47] Arnold S. Tannenbaum, "Control and Effectiveness in a Voluntary Organization," *American Journal of Sociology,* LXVII (1961), 33–47.

[48] *Administrative Science Quarterly,* IV (1959), 43–67. In his *Comparative Analysis of Complex Organizations,* Etzioni relegates authority to the periphery of his conceptual scheme in preference for the concepts of compliance and power; compliance is defined as "a relationship consisting of the power employed by superiors to control subordinates and the orientation of the subordinates to this power." *Op. cit.,* pp. xv, 3. For rather unsatisfactory analytical distinctions between compliance, authority, and "normative" power, see *ibid.,* pp. 14–15.

[49] Etzioni, "Authority Structure . . . ," *op. cit.,* p. 67.

[50] H. Thomas James, "The Nature of Professional Authority," *Phi Delta Kappan,* XLI (November 1959), 45–58; Burton R. Clark, "Faculty Authority," *AAUP Bulletin,* XLVII (Winter 1961), 293–302.

[51] Howard S. Becker, "The Teacher in the Authority System of the Public School," in Etzioni, *Complex Organizations, op. cit.,* pp. 243–251;

Of the increasing number of studies on hospital administration, three articles focusing on authority relations may be mentioned. In a case analysis of relationships between role behavior and social structure in two hospital wards, Coser compares the formal structure of authority with *de facto* lines of decision-making. Bennis and his associates find that none of the satisfactions most desired by hospital nurses could be manipulated by supervisors. Formal authority was relatively ineffective in terms of the rewards it could provide. Bates and White utilize self-administered questionnaires in thirteen voluntary hospitals to record significant differences and potential areas of conflict in perceptions of authority among four hospital groups: board members, administrators, doctors, and nurses.[52]

Perhaps because of the relative ease of access, a number of recent studies—for example, those by Marvick and Weiss—of organizational behavior and administration have taken place in research institutions.[53] Both of the studies emphasize differential perceptions of authority held by professional staff and administrative officials in a federal agency charged with the supervision of research contracts.

Evan and Zelditch have reported the results of a "part-replica" experimental laboratory technique in which attitudes toward bureaucratic authority were examined.[54] Using forty-five college

---

Neal Gross, Ward S. Mason, and Alexander W. McEachern, *Explorations in Role Analysis: Studies of the School Superintendency Role* (New York: John Wiley & Sons, 1957).

[52] Rose Laub Coser, "Authority and Decision-Making in a Hospital: A Comparative Analysis," *American Sociological Review,* XXIII (1958), 56–63; W. Bennis, N. Berkowitz, M. Affinito, and M. Malone, "Authority, Power, and the Ability to Influence," *Human Relations,* XI (1958), 143–155; F. L. Bates and R. F. White, "Differential Perceptions of Authority in Hospitals," *Journal of Health and Human Behavior,* II (1961), 262–267.

[53] Dwaine Marvick, *Career Perspectives in a Bureaucratic Setting,* ("Michigan Governmental Studies," No. 27 [Ann Arbor: Institute of Public Administration, University of Michigan, 1954]); Robert S. Weiss, *Processes of Organization* (Ann Arbor: Survey Research Center, Institute for Social Research, 1956).

[54] William M. Evan and Morris Zelditch, Jr., "Experiment on Bureaucratic Authority," *American Sociological Review,* VI (1961), 883–893. In the "part-replica" technique, organizational ranks are simulated so that subjects think of themselves as participants in a complex organization.

students as subjects, the experimenters systematically varied the technical knowledge of the coding supervisors in a fictitious national research organization and then examined the coder's performance and conformity to rules and commands. Similar experimental techniques are being used in conjunction with field studies of authority relations by a team of Stanford University sociologists including Morris Zelditch and Richard Scott.

Industrial Organizations

Modern organizational theory is primarily a theory of industrial organizations. Most of the empirical studies reviewed by Argyris, March and Simon, Etzioni, Likert, and Blau and Scott have their setting in industrial organizations. Most of them focus on low-level supervisor-worker relationships. Illustrative of the divergent conceptions of authority in this literature are articles by Browne; M. Dalton; Simpson; Stinchcombe; and Barnes, G. Dalton and Zaleznik.[55] Browne reports on the use, as part of the Ohio Leadership studies, of self-administered R, A, and D scales designed to measure degrees of perceived responsibility, authority, and delegation among business leaders. Dalton analyzes conflicts between staff and line officers in an industrial setting, a conflict which reflects diverse bases of authority. Although traditional administrative theory generally holds that communication should and does move vertically through-

---

Morris Zelditch, Jr., and Terence K. Hopkins, "Laboratory Experiments with Organizations," in Etzioni, *Complex Organizations, op. cit.*, pp. 464–478, 474. For contrasting uses of experimental laboratory techniques, see Alex Bavelas, "Communication Patterns in Task-Oriented Groups," in Dorwin Cartwright and Alvin Zander, eds., *Group Dynamics: Research and Theory* (Evanston, Ill.: Row, Peterson, 1953), pp. 493–506.

[55] Clarence G. Browne, "Study of Executive Leadership in Business. I. The R, A, and D Scales," *Journal of Applied Psychology*, XXXIII (1949), 521–526; Melville Dalton, "Conflicts Between Staff and Line Managerial Officers," *American Sociological Review*, XV (1950), 324–351; Richard L. Simpson, "Vertical and Horizontal Communication in Formal Organizations," *Administrative Science Quarterly*, IV (1959), 188–196; Arthur L. Stinchcombe, "Bureaucratic and Craft Administration of Production: A Comparative Study," *Administrative Science Quarterly*, IV (1959), 168–187; Louis B. Barnes, Gene W. Dalton, and Abraham Zaleznik, "The Authority Structure as a Change Variable." Paper presented at the American Sociological Association Convention, Washington, D.C., September, 1962.

out the hierarchy, Simpson finds that communication among first-line foremen of a textile mill was mainly horizontal, cutting across lines of authority. Stinchcombe systematically compares mass-production and construction industries with a resulting modification of Weber's ideal type of bureaucracy. Barnes, Dalton, and Zaleznik analyze the conflict between "knowledge-based" authority and "position-based" authority in the product-development laboratories of a large industrial firm.

Gouldner's *Patterns of Industrial Bureaucracy,* an intensive case study of a gypsum-mining and -processing plant, extends Weber's theory of bureaucracy by developing the distinction between representative- and punishment-centered types, with particular emphasis on the consequences of bureaucratic rules.[56]

Two notable studies of managerial authority in different cultural settings are Elliot Jaques's work in the Glacier Metal Company in England and Heinz Hartmann's survey of management practices in Germany. Jaques defines authority as a quality of the social structure of the organization as distinct from power, a quality of individuals or groups.

> The *authority* attached to a given position in the firm is the statement of what any person (or body) occupying that position can do, whom he can instruct, what equipment he can use, and what he can authorize to be done. In short, the authority system of a community is a formal structure which defines and regulates the means and directions in which individuals or bodies may exert power.[57]

Hartmann distinguishes between functional authority based on technical knowledge, which he maintains is characteristic of American managerial practices, and ultimate authority, where both parties take the superior-subordinate relationship as given, which he argues is more typical of German management practices.[58]

---

[56] Alvin W. Gouldner, *Patterns of Industrial Bureaucracy* (Glencoe, Ill.: Free Press, 1954); see also his *Wildcat Strike* (Yellow Springs, Ohio: Antioch Press, 1954).

[57] Elliot Jaques, *The Changing Culture of a Factory* (London: Tavistock Publications Ltd., 1951), p. 254.

[58] Heinz Hartmann, *Authority and Organization in German Management* (Princeton: Princeton University Press, 1959), pp. 5–7.

A vast number of empirical studies of leadership and control processes, although not always explicitly focusing on authority relations, should also be noted here. The work of only two groups will be singled out—the research findings of the Ohio leadership studies, summarized in works by Shartle and Stogdill,[59] and the extremely important cumulative contributions of Likert, Kahn, Mann, Morse, Pelz, Seashore, Tannenbaum, and others in the human-relations program of the Michigan Survey Research Center, summarized in Likert's *New Patterns of Management*.[60]

Governmental Agencies

Unless one includes military organizations and government research institutions in the category of governmental agencies, studies of organizational relationships in government are relatively rare. Peter M. Blau's contributions, however, deserve extended comment. In his book, *The Dynamics of Bureaucracy*, a study of interpersonal relations in two governmental agencies, Blau devotes one chapter to the exercise of authority in a federal enforcement agency.[61] Heavily influenced by Weber's analysis of bureaucratic authority, Blau also acknowledges the work of Barnard and Simon. Distinguishing between authority willingly accepted and supervisory control coerced through the threat or use of sanctions, Blau suggests that the ultimate source of bureaucratic authority is the official power of sanction, externally bestowed.[62]

In his theoretical monograph, *Bureaucracy in Modern Society*, Blau extends this analysis of authority as follows:

> First, it refers to a relationship between persons and not to an attribute of one individual. Second, authority involves

[59] Carroll L. Shartle, *Executive Performance and Leadership* (Englewood Cliffs, N.J.: Prentice-Hall, Inc., 1956); Ralph M. Stogdill, *Individual Behavior and Group Achievement* (New York: Oxford University Press, 1959).

[60] Rensis Likert, *New Patterns of Management* (New York: McGraw-Hill, 1961). For earlier summaries of research findings, see "Human Relations Research in Large Organizations, I, II," *Journal of Social Issues*, VII, No. 3 (1951), and XII, No. 2 (1956).

[61] *Op. cit.*, chap. xi.

[62] *Ibid.*, pp. 172–178.

exercise of social control which rests on the *willing* compliance of subordinates with certain directives of the superior. He need not coerce or persuade subordinates in order to influence them, because they have accepted as legitimate the principle that some of their actions should be governed by his decisions. Third, authority is an observable pattern of interaction and not an official definition of a social relationship. . . . Actual authority, consequently, is not granted by the formal organization chart, but must be established in the course of social interaction. . . .[63]

This theoretical analysis of authority receives additional support from interview data derived from a 1957 study of a large metropolitan welfare agency by Blau joined with an approximately parallel study by Scott of a county welfare agency in a smaller urban center. The results of these two studies are mixed with a comprehensive review of much of the existing literature on organizational behavior. Working initially from Weber's classic typology, Blau and Scott suggest that "the authority of superiors in a formal organization is legitimated by legal contract rather than by traditional values or by an ideological identification with a charismatic leader."[64] Since formal authority is limited, managers must extend their influence by other means, including leadership. Distinctions were also made between "authoritarian" and "nonauthoritarian" styles of supervision. Contrary to expectations and the findings of other studies, work-group productivity did not seem to be related to authoritarianism.[65]

Military Organizations

Since, as Weber noted, "the modern army is essentially a bureaucratic organization," it is not surprising that military organizations should be prominent field settings for the study of bureaucratic authority.[66] Among such studies, several chapters in *The American Soldier* and a number of journal articles by Campbell and

---

[63] *Op. cit.*, p. 71.
[64] Blau and Scott, *op. cit.*, p. 140.
[65] *Ibid.*, pp. 148–153.
[66] Weber, *Theory* . . . , *op. cit.*, pp. 334–335.

McCormack, Feld, Thompson, and Janowitz may be cited.[67] Of these studies, Mr. Brewster Smith's analysis, "Combat Motivations Among Ground Troups," in the second volume of *The American Soldier* and Morris Janowitz's discussion of changing patterns of organizational authority elaborated on in his study, *The Professional Soldier,* may be singled out for further comment.[68] Smith's analysis of combat incentives named by officers and enlisted veterans suggests the hypothesis that, the higher the position in the organization, the greater the emphasis placed on the importance of authority and sanctions as a means of accomplishing organizational objectives.[69] He also analyzes the role of coercive institutional authority in the army.

In contrast, Janowitz focuses attention on a shift in the characteristic mode of exercising authority—from domination to manipulation. In military establishments, skill in interpersonal relations rather than technical competence is emphasized as the basis of authority.[70] This conclusion receives tentative support in the present study of authority in a military-type organization, a police department (see Chapter VII).

Mental Institutions and Prisons

Although the classifying of mental institutions and prisons under the same category may be somewhat arbitrary, these total institutions have certain characteristics in common, including barricades to interaction with the outside social environment, a single tent of authority enveloping the entire institution, hierarchical

---

[67] Samuel A. Stouffer *et al., The American Soldier* (2 vols.; Princeton: Princeton University Press, 1949), I, chap. viii; II, chap. iii; Donald T. Campbell and T. H. McCormack, "Military Experience and Attitudes Toward Authority," *American Journal of Sociology,* LXII (1957), 482–490; M. D. Feld, "Information, Authority, and Military Organization," *American Sociological Review,* XXIV (1959), 15–22; James D. Thompson, "Authority and Power in 'Identical' Organizations," *American Journal of Sociology,* LXII (1956), 290–301; and Morris Janowitz, "Changing Patterns of Organizational Authority: The Military Establishment," *Administrative Science Quarterly,* III (1959), 473–493.

[68] Morris Janowitz, *The Professional Soldier* (Glencoe, Ill.: Free Press, 1960), Part II.

[69] Stouffer *et al., op. cit.,* II, 108–111.

[70] Janowitz, "Changing Patterns . . . ," *op. cit.,* p. 492.

classes of people (some classes having considerable authority over others), and imposed institutional cultures. Goffman imaginatively develops some of the consequences of these and other characteristics of total institutions, based on impressions of life in a mental hospital from the patient's perspective.[71] Among contrasting views of the hierarchical structures of mental hospitals, the work of Stanton and Schwartz and articles by Henry; Lefton, Dinitz, and Pasamanick; and Mishler and Tropp should be noted.[72]

Among empirical studies dealing with various aspects of the problem of authority in prisons, articles by Cressey, Grusky, Mc-Cleery, and Sykes are instructive.[73] One of the consequences of a shift from custodial to rehabilitative goals may be a shift from a single to a dual hierarchy, with increasing emphasis on professional skills as a base of authority.

[71] Erving Goffman, "Interpersonal Persuasion," in Bertram Schaffner, ed., *Group Processes* (New York: Josiah Macy Jr. Foundation, 1957), pp. 117–118.

[72] Alfred H. Stanton and Morris S. Schwartz, *The Mental Hospital* (New York: Basic Books, 1954); Jules Henry, "The Formal Social Structure of a Psychiatric Hospital," *Psychiatry*, XVII (1954), 139–151; Mark Lefton, Simon Dinitz, and Benjamin Pasamanick, "Decision-Making in a Mental Hospital: Real, Perceived, and Ideal," *American Sociological Review*, XXIV (1959), 822–829; and Elliot G. Mishler and Asher Tropp, "Status and Interaction in a Psychiatric Hospital," *Human Relations*, IX (1956), 187–205.

[73] Donald R. Cressey, "Contradictory Directives in Complex Organizations: The Case of the Prison," *Administrative Science Quarterly*, IV (1959), 1–19; Oscar Grusky, "Role Conflict in Organization: A Study of Prison Camp Officials," *Administrative Science Quarterly*, III (1959), 452–472; Richard McCleery, "Communication Patterns as Bases of Systems of Authority and Power," *Theoretical Studies in Social Organization of the Prison* (New York: Social Science Research Council, 1960), pp. 49–77; and Gresham M. Sykes, "The Corruption of Authority and Rehabilitation," *Social Forces*, XXXIV (1956), 257–262. Sykes has also contributed a theoretical analysis of authority structures which rejects current formal theories in favor of a conceptualization in terms of three components: the areas of action over which authority is exercised, modes of authority, and sequences or "chains of command." "The Structure of Authority," *Public Opinion Quarterly*, XVII (1953), 146–150.

III

An Approach to the Field Study of
Superior-Subordinate Relationships

The research design adopted reflects the exploratory nature of this study. The field phase was undertaken as a means of gaining new insights into a relatively unresearched phenomenon: authority relations in government organizations. Throughout the study, the researcher was confronted with the problem of linking perceptions of authority with behavior. Although the perceptions of people are crucial in understanding what they do and why they do it, it is at least equally important to observe what actually occurs. Knowledge that a person is predisposed to accept authority does not tell us what he actually does about the unacceptable exercise of authority when confronted with it. Furthermore, the congruence of an individual's behavior with his earlier statements about how he would behave always remains problematical. However, the assumption that behavior will depend on the respondent's "definition of the situation," as W. I. Thomas put it, seems to be a valid one.[1] The

[1] "If men define situations as real, they are real in the consequences." W. I. Thomas and D. S. Thomas, *The Child in America* (New York: Alfred

44

decision to spend as much time as possible in the organizations observing routine and crisis behavior and the choice of an interview schedule rather than a self-administered questionnaire were guided by this concern. This problem, as Thomas saw it, was how to study "the objective aspects of social life in a way that is verifiable and at the same time to catch the subjective interpretations of the participants."[2] For, as Alfred Schutz asserts, the essential difference in the structure of the mental constructs formed by the social scientists as contrasted with the natural sciences is that:

> . . . the constructs of the social sciences are, so to speak, constructs of the second degree, namely, constructs of the constructs made by actors on the social scene, whose behavior the social scientist has to observe and to explain in accordance with the procedural rules of his science.[3]

The difficulties encountered in observing authority relations and obtaining perceptions about authority in organizations are hardly less complex than the problem of constructing a viable concept of authority. Review of the literature in an attempt to isolate the most important analytical aspects of the concept convinced the researcher that further clarification was most likely to come from an attempt to link concept-formation with field work. Perhaps the essence of systematic research is the selection of data in terms of working hypotheses and the reconsideration of these hypotheses in terms of the data collected. The three local government organizations were viewed as the field settings within which hypotheses about authority relations could be explored.

This research was not aimed at describing total organizational behavior, nor was it designed to test hypotheses consisting of causal relationships between clearly defined and carefully controlled variables. Even though all the relevant variables cannot be studied simultaneously nor rigorously controlled, the researcher must plunge in somewhere. All observers operate under assumptions which enable

---

A. Knopf, 1928), p. 572. Quoted in Edmund H. Volkart, ed., *Social Behavior and Personality* (New York: Social Science Research Council, 1951), p. 14.

[2] *Ibid.*, pp. 14–15.

[3] Alfred Schutz, "Concept and Theory Formation in the Social Sciences," *Journal of Philosophy*, LI (1954), 267.

them to see some things and prevent them from seeing others. The investigator should make these assumptions as explicit as possible. Hence the decision in this case to begin with the identification of several key variables which seemed to be operating on the acceptance of authority. This stage was followed by an attempt to formulate working hypotheses which, in turn, guided the construction of the interview schedule. Before tracing this process in more detail, one assumption underlying this study needs further comment.

The state of existing knowledge in the field suggested that it would be premature to construct a research design which had as its principal objectives minimizing bias and maximizing the reliability of the evidence collected.[4] Instead, it appeared desirable to seek maximum flexibility permitting broad consideration of as many different aspects of authority relations as possible. In summary, then, this study is *exploratory* rather than *explanatory*. Its central theoretical concern is the description and analysis of organizational authority.

THE INTERVIEW SCHEDULE

The key concepts and working hypotheses developed by researchers evolve from many sources—their own experience, immersion in the literature, but, perhaps most importantly, from the kinds of question they ask as they formulate the research problem. Why do people accept authority in organizations? Why do some people (subordinates) obey the orders of other people (superiors)? More broadly, in what ways should cooperative effort be organized in order to achieve organizational goals *and* individual satisfactions— objectives which are not always compatible? These questions begin to suggest a number of variables, some more central than others, including acceptance of authority, level of position in the hierarchy, individual satisfactions, and organizational goals.

The Development of Indexes

Why begin with these variables and not others? "Obedience,"

---

[4] For a detailed discussion of this problem, see Claire Selltiz, M. Jahoda, M. Deutsch, and S. W. Cook, *Research Methods in Social Relations* (rev. ed.; New York: Henry Holt & Co., 1959), chap. v.

"influence," the "size" or "type of organizations"—these, or an almost unlimited number of variables, could have been selected. In *Organizations,* March and Simon list and attempt to relate over two hundred variables pertinent to organizational behavior.[5] The four selected here—acceptance of authority, level of position in the hierarchy, organizational goals, and individual satisfactions—are as basic as any others to organizational behavior in general and to the immediate research focus: authority relations. Furthermore, they offer further possibilities for the development of operational indicators[6] and the construction of questions which would produce data that the researcher was satisfied to accept as indicators of these concepts. This is not the place to get deeply enmeshed in the philosophical assumptions underlying operational definition. In essence, this approach holds that concepts are given their meaning by the methods of observation or investigation used to arrive at the concepts.[7]

As a general rule, the more abstract the concept, the more difficult it is to isolate acceptable empirical indicators for the concept. Thus it was fairly simple to arrive at indicators for the concept "level of position in the hierarchy." One could begin by examining organizational charts, job specifications, and position classifications. These, in turn, could be correlated with such questions as, "To whom are you responsible?" (Question 6a) and "What are your responsibilities for supervising the work of others?" (Question 10). In organizational settings, supervisors are clearly distinguishable from workers in a number of obvious ways. For example, in military-type organizations, such as a police department, identification is facilitated by insignia worn on the sleeves or shoulders of uniforms.

Concepts like "organizational goals" and "individual satisfactions" are much more diffuse and difficult to make operational.

---

[5] *Op. cit.,* pp. 249–253.

[6] Hempel, *op. cit.;* Paul F. Lazarsfeld and Morris Rosenberg, *The Language of Social Research* (Glencoe, Ill.: Free Press, 1955), sections I and II.

[7] As P. W. Bridgman, the physicist generally accredited with instigating the operational approach, asserts: "In general, we mean by any concept nothing more than a set of operations; *the concept is synonymous with the corresponding set of operations." The Logic of Modern Physics* (New York: Macmillan Co., 1927), p. 5.

Most organizations attempt to formulate organizational goals in the form of policy statements; such was the case in the three organizations studied. Whether perceptions agreed with these formal statements was a matter of empirical determination. Each person was asked to state in his opinion "the two or three most important things that the organization should be doing" (Question 1) and then which of these things was the most important (Question 1a) and why (Question 1b). Respondents were also asked how successful they thought the organization had been in accomplishing its purpose (Question 2). It was hypothesized that, the greater the perceived success of the organization, the stronger the acceptance of authority in the organization. Essentially the same approach was used to develop indicators for job satisfactions—namely, a broad general question followed by several probing questions and an attempt at closure (questions 4, 4a, 4b, and 4c). In general, it was hypothesized that, the higher the individual job satisfaction, the greater his propensity to accept authority in the organization. Some empirical results bearing on these hypotheses are reported in Chapter VI.

The Acceptance of Authority

With the concept "acceptance of authority," as with the other concepts, what at first appears to be a fairly simple construct is seen to refer to a complex combination of phenomena. Acceptance of authority may be contrasted with the alternative notions of rejection at one extreme and behavior in conformity with orders which have been anticipated but not received at the other extreme. The indicators for the acceptance of authority consist of "no" answers to questions asking about conflict-producing instructions and the exercise of authority considered unacceptable (questions 7 and 8). These indicators are admittedly crude, and one of their shortcomings is that a "no" response to questions 7 and 8 can be interpreted in at least two contradictory ways. It may mean, for example, with regard to Question 8, that the superior has not actually exercised his authority in a manner unacceptable to the respondent or, conversely, that the subordinate hesitates to commit himself for fear that his answer will get back to his superior and sanctions will be brought to bear. As Chapter VI develops in detail, this is one of the inevitable limitations of interview questions where one answer is more "respectable" than another. As a consequence, the response with the least possibility of repercussion may sometimes be taken. For complete wording of the interview questions, see the Appendix.

There were also several additional questions to assist in the explanation of another basic question posed earlier—namely, "What determines whether or not a subordinate accepts the authority of his superior?" Initially, three important analytical types of authority relations were postulated: (1) authority of position, (2) authority of competence, and (3) authority of person. The most appropriate index to authority of position was obvious—the incumbent's occupancy of formal office, including job title, in the organization. Responses to Question 14—"When you need some professional advice or assistance, where do you get it?"—were used as an index to authority of competence. An index of authority of person was developed from responses to Question 17—"More specifically, who do you think is a good leader in (name of organization)?" Question 17 followed a question about the qualities or traits making for a "good leader" in the particular organization. A fourth type— authority based on legitimacy—was developed from responses by organizational members and re-examination of the literature. Given these indexes, several working hypotheses relating authority of competence and authority of person to this composite authority of position were advanced:

1. Authority of position is strongest when supported by both authority of competence and authority of person.

1.1 If the immediate superior or superiors are not perceived as a source of professional advice and assistance (authority of competence), then authority of position is weakened.

1.2 If the immediate superior or superiors are not perceived as good leaders in the organization (authority of person), then authority of position is weakened.

2. Conversely, if the immediate superior or superiors are perceived neither as a source of professional advice nor as good leaders, then the absence of these bases of authority

will result in a broakdown of authority of position and the
loss of legitimacy attributed to that position.

In summary, then, the first stage of the research procedure—
formulation of the problem—led to the selection of key variables
and the development of working hypotheses which, in turn, dictated
the kinds of question making up the semistructured interview schedule. The exploratory nature of this study dictated the use of open-
ended or free-response questions in the main. This phase of the
research was spread over a three-month period from late August
to late November, 1959. After considerable modification and revision, a pretest interview schedule was administered to fourteen subjects, members of several organizations, in early December. The
interview schedule was then revised to its present form consisting
of a face sheet containing personal data and eighteen major questions, fourteen of which break down into two or more parts (see
Appendix). The information on the face sheet, obtained from personal records for the most part, consists of such factual items as age,
sex, formal education, previous experience, position, and length of
time in a position and with the organization.

THE FIELD PHASE

Even before working hypotheses were fully formulated and the
interview schedule completed, the investigator faced, first, the problem of selecting the kinds of organization in which to carry out the
field phase of the research and, second, arrangements for access
after this decision had been made. Several possibilities were considered before finally deciding to carry out the field phase in three
local government organizations. These included research in two
or three subdivisions of one large government agency, as, for example, in the administrative office, planning staff, and one of the line
departments of a large council-manager city, or research in two or
three subdivisions of a state or federal regional office. Another
possibility would have been to carry out the research at two or three
levels of government, in the manner of Blau's research in a state
employment agency and federal labor-law-enforcement regional
office.[8] It was further assumed that, since complex organizations

[8] *The Dynamics of Bureaucracy, op. cit.*

consist of aggregates of smaller units, it would not be necessary to conduct interviews throughout the parent organization. As Barnard has observed, "Whatever the nature of authority, it is inherent in the simple organization unit; . . . a correct theory of authority must be consistent with what is essentially true of these unit organizations."[9]

For several reasons, both scientific and practical, three local government suborganizations were selected as the field setting in which hypotheses relating to authority relations were explored. These three organizations—a branch office of a large county welfare department, a police department in a council-manager city of some 25,000 population, and an elementary school in a suburban school district—shared roughly the same broad cultural setting in that all three public agencies were located within a ten-mile radius and operated from overlapping or analogous political, social, and economic bases. The welfare office with twenty-three members, the police department with thirty-three members, and the elementary school with twenty-one members were roughly comparable in size. The hierarchical structure of the police department consisted of five formal ranks (chief, lieutenant, sergeants-inspectors, patrolmen, and dispatchers–clerical staff), the welfare office had four (district director, supervisors, social workers, and clerical staff), and the elementary school had three (principal, teachers, and supporting staff).

The police department was selected as an organization that, at least outwardly, seemed to epitomize reliance on authority of position as exemplified by such characteristics as clear-cut distinctions between ranks and within ranks, the wearing of uniforms, and the use of strict sanctions for disciplinary purposes. In contrast, it was expected that schoolteachers and social welfare workers would, at least in theory, place greater emphasis on professional standards, with a consequent diffusion of authority throughout the hierarchical structure. The ratio of supervisory personnel to rank-and-file workers ranged from one to five in the police department, to one to six in the welfare department, to one to seventeen in the elementary school.[10]

[9] *The Functions* . . . , *op. cit.*, p. 161.
[10] The school principal shared supervisory responsibilities with central

Once the type of organization for the field phase had been selected, arrangements for access proved relatively easy. Each organization was approached by letter or telephone through the top external executive—the county manager, city manager, and school superintendent, respectively. After interviewing and securing initial clearance from these executives, arrangements were made to contact the top internal executives of the three suborganizations under study —the district director, police chief, and school principal. In each case, the top external director first discussed the feasibility of the study with the subordinate, or subordinates, involved before granting his approval. Two or three weeks of preliminary observation were followed by informal and formal interviews with all members of the organizations. Each study included follow-up interviews with key central office personnel and/or the top external executive.

Seventy-six persons were interviewed in the three local government organizations. Formal interviews were held with *all* members of the organizations—top executives, supervisors, workers, and clerical personnel—with the exception of one elderly schoolteacher who declined to participate. These interviews ranged from twenty minutes to three hours, averaging approximately one hour in length. Formal interviews were supplemented by some twenty more-or-less informal interviews held with key administrative and staff personnel in the parent organizations and such materials as organizational charts and manuals, personnel records, and newspaper accounts. Considerable time was also spent observing routine and crisis situations in day-to-day operations, staff meetings, coffee breaks, and informal conferences.

Field experiences in the three organizations varied from seven and eight weeks in the welfare office and police department to four weeks in the elementary school, the last organization observed. At least two and as many as five days a week were spent in the organizations for as many as ten hours a day. All but one interview took place on the job, usually in the building which housed the organization. A number of police department interviews, however, were held in squad cars patrolling beats. In every case, interviews were

---

office personnel over the office secretary, custodian, and school nurse (part time).

held in privacy, usually in a conference room or private office. With every supervisory person, formal interviews were preceded by at least one and usually several informal discussions ranging from a half-hour to several hours in length. To the extent that it was possible, the same procedure was adopted for rank-and-file members. Although every interview was unique to the extent that it involved adjusting to different personalities, each interview followed a fairly typical pattern dictated by the interviewer's opening remarks describing the study and attempting to put the interviewee at ease. Each respondent was assured that the responses would be treated as confidential and that only a summary report of the entire study would get back to the organization. Typewritten copies of the original interview notes, recording as far as possible verbatim responses, served as the basic documents for subsequent classification, coding, and analysis of the interview data. The total field phase extended over a five-month period from late November, 1959, to late April, 1960.

IV

A Police Department, a Welfare Office, and an Elementary School

A municipal police department in Garden City, a welfare department branch office in Orchard County, and an elementary school in Forest Heights School District provide the setting for this field study of authority relations.[1] Each organization will be briefly examined in terms of four considerations: organizational goals, formal structure and membership, informal patterns of behavior, and stages of growth. This institutional description will be neither exhaustive nor detailed. If this study had a different focus, if it were interested in describing total organizational behavior or understanding the particular roles played by individual members, several of these categories would have to be expanded, and further attempts made to link these considerations more systematically.[2] Such is not the purpose of this chapter. Rather, it attempts to provide a back-

---

[1] The proper names of the organizations are pseudonyms used to protect the anonymity of the three organizations and their personnel.

[2] For one attempt, see Chris Argyris, *Understanding Organizational Behavior* (Homewood, Ill.: Dorsey Press, 1960), pp. 82–83.

ground for subsequent chapters which analyze authority relations in some depth and detail.

Before subjecting each organization to more elaborate scrutiny, some repetition may be avoided by summarizing some of the characteristics common to all three organizations. First, as already noted, the organizations are located in adjacent or overlapping local government jurisdictions and thus share fairly similar environments. All three organizations serve middle- and upper middle-class communities for the most part, but all three organizations, in varying degrees, have some contact with lower economic classes. The public welfare agency and police department face a roughly comparable problem with minority groupings. The particular clientele—citizens with complaints and law violators, welfare recipients, school children—differ as do other characteristics of the more particular organizational environment. Some of these differences are elaborated in connection with the analysis of the separate organizations.

Second, the organizations are task-oriented. In other words, employees engage in activities designed to achieve organizational purposes, such as protection of citizens, service to welfare clients, and education of children. These organizational purposes also set limits to the types of structures appropriate for these organizations.

All three organizations are governmental units operating under and enforcing or carrying out the provisions of local, state, and, to a lesser extent, national law. Each organization is governed by a five-member board—the Garden City Council, the Orchard County Board of Supervisors, and the Forest Heights School Board—who, in turn, appoint a general manager to carry out and assist in the formation of policy under state law and local ordinances. These chief executives—the city manager, the county manager, and the school superintendent—in turn, appoint subordinate administrators —departmental heads, such as the police chief, the director, and the school principal—who assist them in carrying out policy and achieving the purposes for which these organizations were created in the first place. The top internal executives and their subordinates are, in turn, responsible for the day-to-day operation of their respective units—the police department, the welfare branch office, the elementary school—and the recruitment, supervision, promotion, and retirement of the subordinates—the rank-and-file workers who carry out the basic tasks. Thus, all of these organizations are characterized by a formal authority structure consisting of related positions with certain attached duties, obligations, and responsibilities.

Another feature the three organizations have in common is people—the incumbents of the formal positions in the authority structure. These people bring with them certain attitudes and pre-dispositions which are conditioned by such factors as sex, age, for-mal education, professional training, and job experience. These individuals are characterized by unique sets of preferences or per-sonalities which interact within the organization. As a result of these interactions, certain informal mechanisms of adjustment be-come institutionalized. Some of these informal patterns of behavior —cliques, coffee-break groups, participative decision-making—are singled out for special comment in order to illustrate some of the dynamics of organizational behavior.

Much still remains to be learned about the relations between the size of an organization and the behavior of its members.[3] All these organizations were small enough so that all members knew each other by name and, with the exception of the police depart-ment with its around-the-clock shifts, each person would probably have a minimum of one or two contacts a week with every other person in the organization.

Finally, each of these organizations is captured at a moment in time. Growth and decline are fundamental to organizations; two of these suborganizations are expanding; one, the elementary school, has reached its optimum size. They vary considerably in the degree of professional maturity and training characteristic of their mem-bership. Throughout the balance of this chapter additional com-parisons will be made.

---

[3] Theodore Caplow, "Organizational Size," *Administrative Science Quarterly*, I (1957), 485–491; Frederic W. Terrien and Donald L. Mills, "The Effect of Changing Size upon the Internal Structure of Organizations," *American Sociological Review*, XX (1955), 11–14; Edwin J. Thomas, "Role Conceptions and Organizational Size," *American Sociological Review*, XXIV (1959), 30–37; Sergio Talacchi, "Organizational Size, Individual Attitudes and Behavior: An Empirical Study," *Administrative Science Quarterly*, V (1960), 398–420.

THE GARDEN CITY POLICE DEPARTMENT

The Garden City Police Department is responsible for law enforcement in a suburban community of approximately 25,000 population. Many of the city's residents commute to and from jobs in a nearby metropolitan center, making Garden City primarily a "bedroom" community. The median family income is considerably above average. Until recently Garden City was fairly quiet by law-enforcement standards. Increasing traffic problems generated by rapid population growth and the problems of preserving peace and order among lower income and minority groups living in a recently annexed area of the city have considerably enhanced the need for a modern, professionally trained police force. Low traffic fatality and accident rates brought about in part by rigorous selective enforcement of traffic laws have given the traffic squad a general "hard-nose" reputation and earned the city several awards from the state traffic safety council.

Organizational Goals

The stated goals of an organization—what it does in fact and what it is and should be doing in the views of its members—are never identical. Organizations vary in the extent to which there is congruency between them. According to the police department manual, which had been drafted and approved by its senior officers, "the work of the police department consists of the preservation of the public peace and order, the apprehension of offenders, the protection of persons and property under the laws of [Western State] and the enforcement of the ordinances of [Garden City]." At the beginning of the interviews, each member was asked what in his opinion were "the two or three most important things that (name of organization) should be doing."[4] Although, as Table 1 suggests,

---

[4] For the complete wording, see Question 1, Appendix. This question was poorly worded. It led to confusion between (1) what the members perceive the organization *is* doing and (2) what they think it *should* be doing. These perceptions should also be distinguished from (3) the stated goals of the organizations as embodied in charters, manuals, or ordinances and (4) what the organization is actually attempting to do. The last question, perhaps the most difficult, can be answered only through techniques of independent observation.

there was general agreement on the preservation of peace and the protection of life and property as important organizational goals, the range of perceived goals was quite diverse. The response of one veteran patrolman may be taken as illustrative:

> The most important, being it's a city police department, is law enforcement, enforcement of the penal code and vehicle code, enforcement and apprehending those involved in it.
> Secondly, aid to actual citizens and people passing through in all manner of ways . . . information, assistance. . . .
> Third, observation of the home area and preventing anything from happening. You cover these three, and that pretty well takes care of it.

Asked to identify the most important purpose of the police department, this patrolman replied:

> You can't have *the* most important. All three simultaneously are important. If I saw a violation in front of me, I would cite it, or a burglar breaking in, I would stop him, or, if a little old lady fell down, I would help her. All three of them go together. It's not a singular job in the police department. Even the specialists, the inspectors, if they saw any one of these three things, they would follow it up.

In general, as Table 1 indicates, the policemen emphasized patrolling, law enforcement, and traffic control as the most important organizational goals.

Formal Structure and Membership

Garden City operates under the council-manager form of government. The city manager, who has been with the city since 1962, first as assistant city manager and since 1958 in his present capacity, is appointed by the city council. He, in turn, appoints the department heads, including the chief of police. A chief, a lieutenant (who is also assistant chief), three sergeants, three inspectors, twenty-one patrolmen, four dispatchers, a police clerk-matron, and the city's switchboard operator are included in the formal hierarchy (see Fig. 2). The two inspectors and one assistant inspector operate on the same level as the sergeants despite quite different assignments. Seven

TABLE 1

PERCEPTIONS OF IMPORTANT ORGANIZATIONAL
GOALS: THE POLICE DEPARTMENT*

Goals	Percentage
Public service, assistance to the public in general	15
Community service, service to the particular community	6
Enforcement of the law, preservation of peace, law, and order	57
Traffic control, accident prevention, and accident investigation	45
Patrolling, crime prevention, protection of life and property	69
Criminal investigation and apprehension	24
Public relations, information services	30
Cooperation with other agencies, the referral of persons to these agencies	3
Minority problems, domestic relations in a particular area	9

* Percentages total more than 100 per cent since respondents were asked to identify two or three of the most important things that the organization should be doing ($N = 33$).

part-time school-crossing guards and a police reserve composed of a lieutenant, three sergeants, and thirteen patrolmen complete the police force roster. These reservists serve in a relief capacity and assist the regulars with special traffic problems created by such activities as athletic contests and the Christmas parade.

The organizational chart, in common with all formal organization charts, can do little more than call attention to the formal positions, job titles, and theoretical links between them. It is made up of straight and unbroken horizontal and vertical lines and uniform sizes of type. Nothing that goes on in organizations is ever quite this straight, uniform, or continuous. The formal chart may indicate authority implied by title and rank, but it does not ensure compliance or hold individuals to the exercise of routine activities. The actual authority relationships may be quite different, as the following three chapters will illustrate.

A police department operates around the clock, seven days a week. Theoretically, patrolmen work a five-day, forty-hour week, although, by the time reports are written up after they come off patrol, their hours may run longer. In general, the patrolmen are divided into three shifts—8:00 A.M. to 4:00 P.M., 4:00 P.M. to 12 A.M., and 12 A.M. to 8:00 A.M.—with some overlapping to take care of special assignments and peak traffic hours. Each shift operates under a shift commander: the lieutenant works the swing shift, the traffic sergeant is also in charge of the day shift, and the other two sergeants rotate the graveyard and relief shifts. While waiting for the vacancy in the sergeant's position to be filled by competitive examinations, the senior officers eligible for the promotion took turns as acting sergeants. Shift assignments for all men other than specialists are rotated every three months. During the past few years there has been increasing specialization. This is reflected not only in the creation of the inspectors' positions, but also by such special duties as the police court liaison officer, the safety patrol officer, traffic squad specialists, and the "Beat 4" operation—the one district in Garden City which had more than its share of disturbances of the peace.

Of the thirty-one men and two women who make up the Garden City Police Department, thirteen have attended college (two of these have college degrees, both in police administration). Almost half of the thirty-three members belong to one or more professional organizations, such as the Police Officers' Association. The median age for all members is thirty-two years. About two-thirds of the police force are married.

Over a third of the members, including all of the supervisory staff, have been with the police department for six years or more. Two-thirds of the force have had six years or more of relevant experience, including service with the military police. The median for total relevant experience both inside and outside this department is approximately seven years. However, a fifth of the force, including the four dispatchers, have been with this department less than six months.

The average patrolman is twenty-eight years old, a high school graduate with possibly a year of college, and, as likely as not, married. He entered police work after three or four years of military service. Since then he has had approximately three years of police

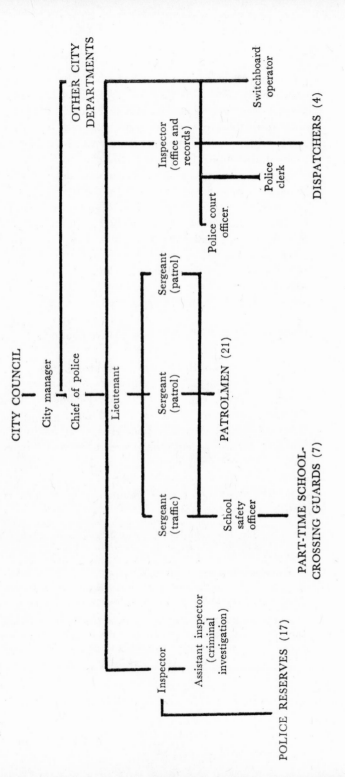

Fig. 2

Organization of Police Department

experience, all of it with the Garden City Police Department. Although he admits that much of police work is routine, the occasional flare of excitement appeals to him. He eventually hopes to move up in the ranks. As one patrolman puts it: "I don't want to remain a patrolman all my life, but then I don't have any visions of being attorney general of [Western State] either."

The supervisory staff of the police department—the chief, lieutenant, two sergeants, and three inspectors—fits a fairly common pattern among police departments of this size. Two are in their middle thirties, the others are in their early or middle forties. All have been promoted from the ranks. Only two had substantial police experience elsewhere before joining the department. Their length of service in the organization ranges from eight to seventeen years. Only one of the seven ranking officers has attended college, although all but one have participated in a number of police-training schools. The chief, who worked his way up through the ranks, is a graduate of the Federal Bureau of Investigation's Police Academy.

Informal Patterns of Behavior: Friendship Cliques

In addition to that most apparent group in organizations—the command group composed of the superior and his immediate subordinates—there are a number of additional groups which can be distinguished, including friendship groups.[5] In any organization one can expect to find a multitude of friendship groups representing the diverse interests of the workers. As Sayles suggests, the boundaries of these clusterings may reflect such off-the-job interests as golfing or horseback riding or such common traits as age, ethnic background, and marital status.

> The friendship group has emerged as the agency which welds the individual to the organization. Loyalty, even attachment, to the total organization with its impersonality, extended hierarchy, and social distance becomes ambiguous. However, attachment to the immediate and easily perceived face-to-face group is the predominant reality of organization

[5] Leonard R. Sayles identifies at least four important groups in organizations: the command group, which is the focus of the present study; the functional or task group; the friendship clique; and the interest group. See his article in Arensberg *et al., op. cit.,* pp. 131–145.

experience. For the individual it provides a source of personal security in an impersonal environment.[6]

The predominant friendship clique in the police department appears to be organized around one of the most experienced and respected ranking officers. A number of junior officers, most of them professionally oriented, look to him as a source of wisdom in police matters as well as personal problems. Several consider themselves to be his protégés. In most cases, the friendship off the job does not seem to lead to an abuse of the relationship on the job. This may be explained in two ways. First, the ranking officer demonstrates strong leadership characteristics which enable him to maintain necessary social distance on the job. Furthermore, the friendship patterns are not so much those between equals as between father and son. As do most of the ranking officers when disciplinary action is required, this man follows the practice of having a personal heart-to-heart conference with individuals before submitting their names on report. This practice has become institutionalized to the extent that, when the patrolmen see this ranking officer with another patrolman under a particular tree beside the station, they purposely stay away, knowing that the individual is probably being reprimanded.

In a profession where reliance on the proper action of your fellow officer may mean the difference between life and death, such friendship relationships or lack of them may be crucial. The importance of protecting one's fellow officer is much more strongly felt and more frequently articulated among the five or six officers most highly identified with this friendship clique. Of course, such cliques are not without certain dysfunctions. Officers on the outside clearly resent this clique, to the point of bitterness. Others imply that it leads to a certain amount of favoritism. Several minority and rival friendship clusters exist, in part organized around other ranking officers. Occasionally, these clusters affect "who gets what there is to get"—for example, the specialist assignments.

These friendship cliques were not nearly so apparent or influential in the other two organizations in which observations were carried out. As Lipset points out, some jobs handicap workers in

[6] *Ibid.,* p. 133.

maintaining adequate off-the-job relations with other friends because of their unusual working hours. These workers—actors, musicians, printers, and policemen—tend to form more closely knit fellow-worker groups.[7]

Stages of Growth

When the present chief of police assumed office in 1948, Garden City had a population of under 10,000, and its police force consisted of one sergeant, five patrolmen, and one clerk. Five years later the city had more than doubled in population, in part owing to annexations, and the police department kept pace. With the creation of the positions of lieutenant and inspector, the force numbered nineteen men. By 1960, the police department included thirty-three members, an increase of over 300 per cent during that twelve-year period. Within the next five years it is expected that several new positions will be added, including a captaincy, another lieutenancy, and several additional sergeant and inspector positions.

Despite this growth rate, the chances of any one patrolman rising in the ranks are not particularly good. For example, under the present chief's administration there have only been five incumbents in the three positions of sergeant. Vacancies occur only when a new position is created, a man is promoted, someone retires, or a person is reduced in rank or dismissed. Thus, when vacancies do occur, competition is keen. The minimum qualifications for the position of sergeant are United States citizenship, good physical condition, and a minimum of five years experience, at least two of which must be with the Garden City Police Department.

One sergeancy position was filled while the police department was under observation. Six patrolmen met the minimum qualifications and took the written examinations sent down from the state capital. Five candidates passed the written examinations and met with the city's personnel board and the assistant city manager for the oral examination. Each man had served as acting sergeant for at least a month prior to the exams and a report of his performance

    [7] Seymour M. Lipset, "The Political Process in Trade Unions: A Theoretical Statement," in Berger, Abel, and Page, *op. cit.*, pp. 101–102.

together with the semiannual efficiency ratings and the police chief's over-all observations were submitted to the personnel board. Three of the candidates were certified as eligible for promotion; one was finally promoted to the sergeancy.

During the course of this study each member was asked about the competition and who he thought would be promoted. Of the fifteen members who were willing to commit themselves on the outcome, over half were correct in their surmise, including all three of the ranking officers who indicated their first choice. The candidates themselves were the ones most likely to distort reality; being the closest and most involved, it could hardly be otherwise.

No matter which candidate was finally selected, he faced as difficult a period ahead as any in his career. Not only was he likely to have frequent contact with his five former competitors, he would also have to deal with their friends and supporters on the force. As one of the experienced officers, but one who was not yet eligible for the competition, put it:

> You find out how they do on the job. It's a big jump. Everybody's looking for them to prove themselves. There are six men up, and only one gets it. You've got to do the job. You've got the brass looking down, and the patrolmen looking up. That's one of the toughest six months for anyone in the department.

This promotional process has been reported in some detail as these and other common processes of all organizations, such as recruitment and decision-making, suggest alternative approaches to the comparative study of organizations.

THE ORCHARD COUNTY WELFARE OFFICE

The second organization to be described—the northern branch office of the Orchard County Welfare Department—has also undergone considerable growth and promotions from the ranks. The branch office, like its parent department, is responsible for administering financial assistance and related social, medical, and rehabilitative services for needy children, the aged, the disabled, and the blind. Its twenty-three members are responsible for over 1,000 cases, or about one-sixth, of Orchard County's old-age-security (OAS)

cases and for approximately 320 cases, or about one-eighth, of fami-
lies on the aid-to-needy-children (ANC) program. This branch
office, one of two in the county, was created in the fall of 1955 to
administer to the needs of several suburban communities. It is
located some twenty miles from the central office of the welfare
department. Staff turnover per year, which ran as high as 25 per
cent in this county but was almost nil in the branch office, and the
shortage of professionally trained workers, which was particularly
acute at this branch, are among major problems facing almost all
county welfare departments.

Organizational Goals

In general, the two major purposes of the welfare department
are to provide services and economic assistance to their clientele,
but there has been a trend away from mere financial support and
limited services. Top executives emphasize the importance of concentrating on underlying problems of dependency in order to get
people off public welfare rolls, thus safeguarding public funds while
rehabilitating human resources. These goals may be compatible in
theory, but they are sometimes difficult to reconcile in practice. As
one top-ranking welfare department executive puts it, "In the long
run, the best welfare program is one which tries to get itself out of
business by helping solve the problems for which it was created."
In the short run, this requires more and better-trained staffs. However, state legislatures and county boards of supervisors are frequently reluctant to assume these costs.

As Table 2 indicates, by far the dominant organizational goal
perceived as important by the members is service to clientele, with
emphasis on the rehabilitation of welfare recipients. Nineteen of the
twenty-three members identified this as important. When asked to
clarify the nature of this organizational goal, a distinct cleavage develops between those members oriented toward services and rehabilitation and those workers who emphasize the importance of
financial assistance. The following excerpts from interviews with
two experienced social workers, neither of them having had
any graduate training in social work, illustrate the diversity of
orientations:

Table 2
Perceptions of Important Organizational Goals: The Welfare Office*

Goals	Percentage
Public service, assistance to the public in general	9
Community service, service to the particular community	26
Enforcement of eligibility, state laws, rules and regulations, the manual	17
Service to welfare recipients, rehabilitation of clientele	83
Financial assistance to and support of welfare recipients	35
Public relations, interpretation of welfare policy, information services	22
Cooperation with other agencies, the referral of people to these agencies	22
Obligation to taxpayers	9
Staff satisfaction as an end in itself	9

* Percentages total more than 100 per cent since respondents were asked to identify two or three of the most important things that the organization should be doing ($N = 23$).

INTERVIEWER: In your opinion, what are the two or three most important things that the welfare branch office should be doing?

SOCIAL WORKER A: . . . I think the most important thing is helping people, helping people in stress or need, to work out, to solve, their problems . . . work them out to the best of their potential or ability . . . helping him to his highest potential. It might be only to support him through his distress. Of course, I think the first important thing is to diagnose this—the individual who comes to us in his period of stress. We plan how we can help him. We plan how he can change, both in the short term and long term. Ultimately our aim is to get him working to his highest potential. Rehabilitation is probably an important word. His highest potential no matter whether it is economic or social or psychological. Help him to lead a happier and more creative life.

In contrast, compare the following response:

SOCIAL WORKER B: Do you want the stock answers? Services,

community contacts, etc.? The advantages of the branch office are not just mainly all for them, the clients. It makes it easier for us to check up on them. . . . Here you can call five or six times on the phone; it's easier to get the people.

INTERVIEWER: Which of these things do you think is the most important?

SOCIAL WORKER B: Seeing that they get everything they're entitled to, not a penny more nor a penny less. The closeness to the job helps here.

These differing viewpoints and the sometimes contradictory interpretations of organizational goals at various levels of the hierarchy illustrate Barnard's distinction between the specific purposes of subunits and the general purpose of the organization as a whole.[8] Furthermore, as Simon points out:

The means-ends hierarchy is seldom an integrated, completely connected chain. Often the connections between organizational activities and ultimate objectives is [sic] obscure, or these ultimate objectives are incompletely formulated, or there are internal conflicts and contradictions among the ultimate objectives, or among the means selected to attain them.[9]

Thus, although top executives may stress the importance of concentrating on underlying problems of dependency *and at the same time* emphasize the need to safeguard public funds, the social worker in the field may emphasize services to the clientele *or* financial assistance, without linking these intermediate objectives to the broader goals of the organization as a whole. Simon's comments regarding the means-ends hierarchy are as applicable to the police department and the elementary school as they are to the welfare branch office. One of the primary functions of the executives in all of these organizations is to attempt to bring about these reconciliations.

Formal Structure and Membership

Although the major programs of the county welfare department are specified by state law, the general plan of execution pro-

---

[8] Barnard, *The Functions* . . . , *op. cit.*, p. 137.
[9] *Administrative Behavior, op. cit.*, p. 64.

vides for local administration of the various programs under the review, supervision, and consultation of the state government's department of social welfare. County boards of supervisors are the responsible local governing bodies, but they delegate much of the administrative policy determination either through county executives to welfare department directors, as in this county, or directly to the welfare directors and their staffs.

A welfare director heads the Orchard County Welfare Department and reports directly to the county manager. The district director, who is responsible for the operation of the two branch offices, reports directly to the welfare director, as do central office division heads and staff. Under the district director's supervision at the northern branch office are two social work supervisors, twelve social workers, a clerical work supervisor, six clerical workers, and a licensing worker for foster homes attached from the central office. The branch office itself is subdivided into three working units: an old-age-security and general-public-assistance (GPA) unit, an aid-to-needy-children unit, and the clerical section which serves the two social welfare units (see Fig. 3).

Of the one male (the district director) and twenty-two females who make up the membership of the welfare office, only three have had graduate training in social work, and only the director holds a master of arts degree. Although a college degree is a job requirement, only two social workers have undergraduate majors in sociology or psychology. Three of the six clerical workers have had one or two years of college; the balance of the clerical staff, including the supervisor, graduated from high school. Only six of the twenty-three-member staff belong to one or more professional organizations. The median age for all members is forty-one years. All but two members of the staff are married; about half of them have children.

What this welfare office lacks in professional training, it makes up, in part, in experience. All but three people have been with the welfare department for two or more years. Nine of the sixteen people making up the professional staff have had relevant social welfare experience outside the agency. The median for total relevant experience both inside and outside this agency is approximately five years.

Fig. 3

ORGANIZATION OF WELFARE OFFICE

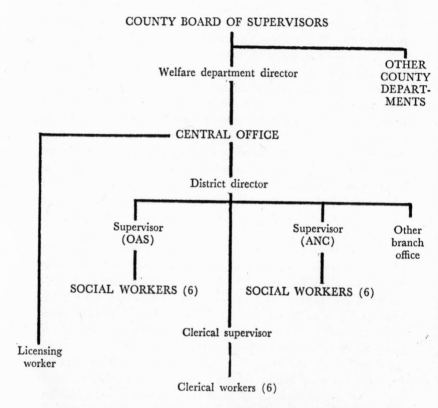

Two typical workers may be suggested for this agency's person-nel. She is either in her late twenties or early forties, married, a col-lege graduate but without formal training in social work. She entered social work directly out of college in the case of the younger workers or, in the case of the older workers, after rearing a family. Two-thirds of the older workers have been teachers at one time. The younger workers have approximately three years of experience, almost all of it with the branch office. The older workers have five to twenty years experience, both in and out of the agency. Both see in social work an opportunity for service *and* additional income for the family. Neither is particularly interested in becoming a supervisor.

The supervisory staff—the director, two social work supervisors, and the clerical supervisor—is even more difficult to fit into a common pattern. Three are in their middle forties; one is over sixty. Their combined experience is broad and varied. The oldest supervisor has been with the welfare department almost thirteen years, the district director not quite three years, and the other two supervisors about five years each. The district director's experience includes some ten years with the federal government and seven years in county welfare work in another state. The two social welfare supervisors were promoted from the ranks, one having served as an intake worker under the other before her promotion. The clerical supervisor lacks the formal rank and prestige of the other supervisors.

Informal Patterns of Adjustment: The Coffee Break

Numerous examples of the ways in which individual personalities interact within the formal structure to create certain informal patterns of adjustment and adaptation could be described. Only one example will be detailed here, namely, the various coffee-break routines in the welfare office. The regulations provide for two fifteen-minute breaks, one in the morning and one in the afternoon. These breaks are staggered among the members to provide continuous coverage of the desks and telephones.

A member of the organization can take her coffee break in the building in a small interior room, complete with several cots and chairs, set aside for this purpose, or she can leave the building and drive to a restaurant about two blocks from the building. The majority of the workers, particularly the clerical personnel, prefer the informal atmosphere and inexpensive coffee prepared in their own lounge. Typical conversations cover a wide range of topics, from family problems to vacation plans and "buys," as well as occasional shop talk. Not only does the coffee break provide an opportunity to get away from the routine of the job, it also helps solve minor disagreements and misunderstandings. As one worker commented:

> Sometimes we'll kid one another when we go to lunch or at coffee break or will talk some problem over. Somebody will say, "Oh, you're no friend of mine. . . ," and it'll go on from there.

The workers who leave the premises during the relief period are a minority, but a fairly consistent group. Two or three close friends or as many as four or five at one time may go out together "just to get away from this place." One fairly consistent friendship clique cutting across the formal divisions in the agency consists of one of the supervisors, two or three social workers, and one of the clerical workers. The small talk among this group is likely to be professionally oriented. A social worker may use the group as a sounding board for a particularly difficult case problem, or ways to get around a trying regulation may be devised.

Perhaps a major value in leaving the building, particularly for the people who go alone or with one other worker, is therapeutic. As one welfare worker put it:

> When the front desk gets crowded, as in the rainy season, and the people . . . and seven typewriters are going—here you are, trying to concentrate, and the telephones are ringing, there's constant traffic back and forth, and the receptionists are yelling at the social workers in the back. . . . The typewriters, the constant tramping—it's thoroughly exhaustive after a day. It's not the job, but the physical setup. . . . If it gets too bad, then I go for a cup of coffee up to [Restaurant X] or out on a field visit.

At other times, this same worker and other employees may go without coffee breaks in order to get the work out.

Stages of Growth

The welfare branch office began operation in the fall of 1955 in one large room with one supervisor, six case workers, and several clerical workers. In four years it has more than doubled its staff and floor space. In another two years it will move into a new building which it will share with the county health services and court officials. Its supervisory staff has grown from one supervisor to three supervisors and a director who is shared with the other branch office. Among the consequences of such a growth pattern are the enhancement of promotional opportunities and reduction of the dangers of losing one's job. However, in terms of individual satisfaction, there may be offsetting inconveniences in bureaucratic growth. The experience of one social worker illustrates this as she compares her relationship with the present top administrator in the welfare department with the top administrator when she first joined the department five years before:

> As far as the main authority—[Mr. D]—I hardly know he exists. When we went up to the main office meeting and this man started talking, I asked who he was, and they said, "He's the director." I didn't know. Whatever they do up there doesn't really affect me. We have so many things to do here.
>
> When [Mrs. E] was director—such a difference. My father gave me an airline ticket to go to Hawaii for two weeks. I couldn't get the time off now if something like that came up. But then I took it to [Supervisor A] and she said, "Why don't you ask [Mrs. E]?" So I went over to her house, and she invited me in for coffee, and she worked it out. Maybe she took too much interest in people, but for the workers it was wonderful. She spent all her time trying to please people. The department was so small at the beginning that she could take the time. She had the social workers at heart—her case load was the workers. It was good from the workers' point of view.

With increasing size, this organization probably will be characterized by greater social distance between superiors and subordinates and increasing reliance on formal rules and regulations rather than informal persuasion. In contrast, the final organization to be described, the Roosevelt Elementary School, appears to have reached optimum size.

THE ROOSEVELT ELEMENTARY SCHOOL

Roosevelt Elementary School is one of twenty-two grade schools, three junior high schools, and two high schools in the Forest Heights Unified School District. This school district operates under the K 6-3-3 plan. Kindergarten and the first six grades meet in one building, the junior high students meet in a separate building, and grades ten through twelve meet in the senior high school. With seventeen classrooms and 515 students Roosevelt Elementary School is somewhat larger than the average elementary school in the district. It serves an area with a radius of approximately one-half mile so that all children are within walking distance.

Organizational Goals

In common with most school districts across the nation, this system has been faced with two major and continuous problems— (1) revision and upgrading of the curriculums to meet increasing demands and changing educational needs and (2) the provision of classrooms for the unprecedented number of students. Even before the impact of Sputnik, public demands had spurred a reappraisal of the nation's education systems, resulting in a tightening up of curriculums and increased attention to instructional processes. During the past decade, the Forest Heights School District has grown from 5,400 pupils to more than 14,000, and the number of schools has increased from twelve to twenty-seven.

As the school district policy manual states, the prime purpose of the schools "is to develop as fully as possible the intellectual faculties of each pupil, and to prepare him for a contributing part in our society." In addition to this twofold purpose, the school district recognizes that some subordinate goals are justified. However, as this statement of objectives continues, "the public schools are not primarily responsible for those aspects of child growth and training traditionally assigned to the home, the church, and the community."

How do these stated objectives compare with the perceptions of the members of Roosevelt Elementary School as to the most important organizational goals? All but two members agree that development of the intellectual faculties through emphasis on the basic skills is among the most important, but emotional adjustment of the child is mentioned by more members than is preparation for citizenship and contributions to society (see Table 3). Some teachers see all three goals as equally important:

> I feel that every one here is dedicated to educating the

child to fit into the society we live in, the world and its advancements. Also, I feel that everyone believes in the skills, the basic fundamental skills of reading, writing, and arithmetic. And also that they should receive character training—training in getting along with others. Citizenship, honesty, consideration for others, respect for others. . . .

TABLE 3

PERCEPTIONS OF IMPORTANT ORGANIZATIONAL GOALS: THE ELEMENTARY SCHOOL*

Goals	Percentage
Public service, assistance to the public in general	5
Community service, service to the particular community	5
Enforcement of the state educational code, the philosophy of the school district	0
Emotional development of the child, psychological adjustment	55
Development of intellectual faculties, education in the basic skills	90
Citizenship, preparation of child for contribution to society	35
Public relations, interpreting policy to the public	5
Staff development, professional standards and training	10
Parent-teacher relationships	45

* Percentages total more than 100 per cent since respondents were asked to identify two or three of the most important things that the organization should be doing ($N = 20$).

But contrast the basic-skill orientation of Teacher A with the emotional-adjustment orientation of Teacher B in the following two excerpts:

TEACHER A: The most important thing is to instruct the children. . . . To do the best possible job of challenging each child to the utmost of his capacity.

TEACHER B: I feel that the most important . . . it's hard to say. I feel very strongly that the school should meet the emotional needs of the child. No matter what problems he has or what they are. Of course, the school isn't qualified to handle severe psychological problems.

When asked to select the most important organizational function, a majority emphasize the basic skills, with about half as many identifying emotional adjustment of the child as the most important. Nine teachers also emphasize the importance of good parent-teacher relationships.

Formal Structure and Membership

In common with the other two organizations studied, the Forest Heights School District is governed by a five-member elective board. The chief executive of the board, the school superintendent, has been head of this school district since 1950. Appointed by the board, he, in turn, is responsible for appointing the principals of the various schools under his supervision. The internal formal hierarchy of each elementary school in the district is standardized and simple. Each school staff consists of a three-level hierarchy: the principal, from ten to seventeen teachers, and the supporting staff (a school secretary and one or two custodians). Several visiting professionals, such as the speech therapist and school nurse, divide their time among four elementary schools (see Fig. 4). The custodian, school nurse, and visiting teachers operate under dual supervision, in the sense that each is responsible to a supervisor in the central office as well as to the principal. Roosevelt Elementary School, the largest in the district, has seventeen teachers, sixteen of whom were interviewed. In addition, interviews were conducted with the principal, secretary, custodian, and school nurse. Class sizes range from twenty to twenty-nine students in the kindergarten and first grades to as high as thirty-three students in the upper grades.

Of the seven men and thirteen women who make up the staff of the Roosevelt Elementary School, 75 per cent have graduate training, including nine members who have the equivalent of a masters degree or beyond. Only three members of the professional staff, all younger teachers, do not have at least one semester of graduate work in education. The two remaining members, the secretary and custodian, are high school graduates or the equivalent. This staff has an extremely high educational background, and all of the professional members of the staff belong to two or more professional organizations.. The median age of the staff, thirty-two years,

Fig. 4

ORGANIZATION OF ELEMENTARY SCHOOL

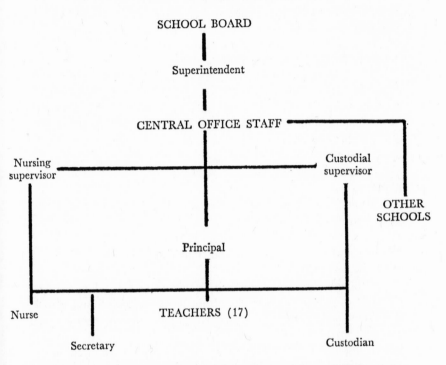

SCHOOL BOARD

Superintendent

CENTRAL OFFICE STAFF

Nursing supervisor

Custodial supervisor

OTHER SCHOOLS

Principal

Nurse

TEACHERS (17)

Secretary

Custodian

is the same as the police department. All but four members of the staff are married.

For five teachers, this was their first year at this school, although two of these five have taught elsewhere, including one who has been a principal. Eight members, including the principal, secretary, and custodian have been with Roosevelt Elementary School for six or more years. The median for total relevant experience both inside and outside this school is approximately six years.

This school has such a diversified faculty in terms of age and experience that it is difficult to characterize the average teacher. Two typical groupings predominate, one consisting of younger women teachers, about two-thirds of them unmarried, a year or two out of college, with perhaps a summer semester of graduate work. The other grouping consists of teachers in their thirties, half of them men, with most of the latter considering an administrative career or already having some experience as a principal before coming to this school district. This group has an average of six or seven years of teaching, and almost all of them have the equivalent of a master's degree or beyond in education.

The principal of the school is forty-two years old and working on his doctorate in education. He has been principal for seven years. Prior to his promotion, he taught for four years in the school. His method of administration is that of a group leader rather than a director; he is inclined toward democratic, if not laissez-faire, leadership rather than autocratic command. One example of these leadership techniques is discussed below. The relation of these techniques to the school environment and the philosophy of administration practiced by the school superintendent is elaborated upon in the following chapters.

Informal Patterns of Behavior: Staff Participation in Decision-Making

Although the formal authority structure of this school system is clear-cut, descending as it does from the school board and school superintendent through the principal to the teachers, decisions as to major goals activities—what, how, and when to teach—may be highly dispersed. This diffusion of authority may be even more characteristic of more highly professionalized organizations, such as research institutions, laboratories, universities and hospitals.[10] In general, it may be hypothesized that, the more professionally oriented the workers, the greater the degree of self-determination exercised by the individual members. This proposition may be illustrated by the manner in which the members of the Roosevelt Elementary School agreed to participate in this study.

As with the other two organizations, initial contact was made with the top executive, in this case, the school superintendent. As with the other two organizations, he first made a point of securing

[10] Etzioni, "Authority Structure . . . ," *op. cit.*

approval from the top administrator of the suborganization in which interviews were to be conducted. Arrangements for access were taken one step further in the school system, however. After the principal agreed to the study in the presence of the superintendent, he suggested that the researcher attend the weekly staff meeting of the elementary school the following morning. Prior to the staff meeting the principal had expressed some misgivings as to the time his staff members would lose. Not only had they participated in a district-wide staff satisfaction survey, but teacher-parent conferences were to begin in two weeks. The atmosphere of the staff meeting was quite informal. While several routine announcements were made, the seventeen teachers and principal sat in easy chairs or around a table drinking coffee and eating sweet rolls. After the principal related how he had been contacted by the school superintendent and gave a brief description of the proposed study, he introduced the researcher. After four or five minutes of further explanation and several questions from teachers, the researcher was asked to leave the room so that a discussion and vote could take place.

It was later revealed that only one teacher, an elderly woman who subsequently refused to be interviewed, had voiced serious objection to the study, although several teachers were concerned about the amount of time it would take. During the formal interview with the principal the following week, his technique of securing staff acceptance was discussed. As he put it:

> . . . You have to have a belief or faith in the outcome of things. . . . I said to them, "You've all done research papers; you know what to expect." I had a hunch that they would go along with it and that this way they would be more cooperative.

The principal's philosophy of administration, based on group participation in decisions, reflects both the superintendent's philosophy and the professional environment. Although this is only one illustration of a number of group decisions that were observed, it seemed fairly typical. It becomes more significant when placed in juxtaposition with decision-making from the top down which seemed to be more characteristic of the other two organizations studied.

Stages of Growth

Since 1950, the school population of the Forest Heights Unified School District has almost tripled, and the number of schools has more than doubled. Throughout this period, despite the growth, an attempt has been made to restrict the size of elementary schools to fourteen classrooms housing about 450 students. The board of education feels that this size is large enough to provide a maximum educational program and small enough to maintain individuality. With its seventeen teachers and 515 pupils, Roosevelt Elementary School has been operating at its maximum capacity for the past several years. Unlike the welfare office and police department, which will both move to new buildings to overcome growth problems, this elementary school will be forced to restrict its boundaries, thus keeping its student population fairly stable. New schools in the area will eventually be built to absorb the increased population.

One pronounced dissimilarity between the welfare office and police department on the one hand and the elementary school on the other is the difference in the degree of professionalization achieved by these organizations. Whereas the former two organizations are beginning to attract trained workers and are placing ever increasing emphasis on in-service training programs, the elementary school seems to have reached its peak as far as attracting graduate-trained teachers. This school district will probably undergo an increasing search for and dependence on professionally trained educational administrators; more militant and unionlike activities on the part of the teachers' associations in behalf of higher wages; and increasing central office control and curriculum standardization over heretofore fairly autonomous schools and classrooms.

SIMILARITIES AND DIFFERENCES

A number of similarities between these three organizations have already been touched on in both the introductory remarks to this chapter and the three sections devoted to institutional description. It remains to pull some of these common characteristics together as well as to point up important differences. To begin, despite their common culture and the fact that all three are local governmental subunits, each deals with distinctly different clientele as they carry out their different purposes. The social worker who refuses to grant a welfare client further assistance or a schoolteacher who finds it necessary to discipline a recalcitrant child may on occasion be confronted with a rejection of his external authority vis-à-vis his particular clientele, but rarely does this lead to threats of physical force. In contrast, as the following excerpts illustrate, the policeman is frequently faced with violence:

> . . . One of the patrolmen was shaking this guy down, and a pistol fell to the ground. A friend of his picked it up and said, "I'm going to get me a cop. . . ."

> . . . The last time I faced a man down with a shotgun, it turned out to be unloaded, but we didn't know it at the time. He pumped it and pulled the trigger. . . . They had to put twenty-seven stitches in his head after I rapped him.

> . . . I drove around the side of the building and there was this fellow standing with his back to me, reaching into the trunk of a blue Plymouth. I flashed the spot on him and told him to turn around. When he didn't answer, I knew I was on to something hot. That's when I made my mistake. The first thing I should have done was radio for cover. As I got out of the right side of the car and was reaching for my gun, somebody came out of the ditch and hit me from behind with a piece of pipe. . . . When I came to, my hands were handcuffed behind me, and my tie had been knotted so tight around my throat they had to cut the tie off. . . .

Certainly such instances are the exception rather than the rule. Anyone who rides in a patrol car cruising a beat late at night or participates in a stake-out for burglars can testify to the fixed routines, if not sheer boredom, characteristic of much police activity. However, these examples point up the obvious, namely, that the expected behavior and training which make for a "good cop" are quite different from those demanded in a social worker or a schoolteacher.

Furthermore, these differences in purpose, clientele, personal characteristics, and training are compounded by the general attitudes held by the public with regard to the membership of these three organizations. Policemen are quite conscious of an ambivalent attitude held by many citizens—a lack of respect mixed with fear of authority.

> People resent not you, but what you represent—the super-parent, so to say. They don't resent you personally, but it's hard to divorce yourself—he's mad at your badge, the city, and the state. When you're involved in enforcement, you have to remember that. It's not you personally he resents, although he may take it out on you as if it were.

Another significant difference in these three organizations is the number of levels in the formal authority structure. The elementary school has only three; the welfare branch office, four; and the police department, five. These levels are further stratified by prestige and salary differentials between line workers and those performing supportive functions, such as the clerical personnel. Length of service and experience also enter in, particularly in the police department, where seniority frequently substitutes for rank. When no commanding officer is present, the senior officer takes charge. A possible source of conflict in all these organizations is brought to the surface whenever a person in a lower-prestige position is able to withhold services or reverse the flow of communications. The transcriber who types for more than one social worker, or the rookie dispatchers who order senior officers to different assignments are likely to engender such conflicts.

Differences in sex, age, formal education, and professional training among the membership of these three organizations have already been noted. Certain rough measures of comparison between organizations as to perceived job satisfaction and organization success, derived from rating scales in the interview schedule, should be commented upon, however. All three organizations score roughly the same on an index of perceived job satisfaction: the welfare office and the elementary school having the same rating, 4.3; the police department scored slightly higher, 4.4. The elementary school scored somewhat lower on an index of perceived organizational success, 4.1, as compared to the 4.3 ratings achieved by the welfare office and police department.[11] In general, these indexes suggest that the

[11] The index of job satisfaction was determined by asking respondents to rate themselves on a scale ranging from one ("very dissatisfied") to five

members of these organizations perceived themselves as "fairly well satisfied" with the job and rated their organizations "fairly successful" compared with similar organizations in the area. Schoolteachers were likely to be somewhat more critical in their judgments of organizational success as compared with other schools in the district.

("very well satisfied"). The index was then derived by multiplying each weight (from one to five) by the number of respondents in each category and dividing this sum by the total number of respondents. The index of organizational success was arrived at in the same manner. (For the complete wording of these questions, see questions 2b and 4c, Appendix.)

V

Perceptions of Authority
and Responsibility

A review of the literature on authority might lead to several such classifications as those developed in Chapter II. However, such classifications and their underlying characteristics do not necessarily reflect the ways in which participants in organizations tend to view or define the relationships to which the words authority and responsibility are but shorthand terms. As David Easton has observed:

> . . . We cannot assume that the average person views the world through the conceptual lenses of the social scientist. The task for the social scientist, then, is to put himself behind the lenses of those persons whose perceptions he is exploring.[1]

The student of organizational behavior must seek to discover just what members of an organization mean when they use words like authority and responsibility and how these meanings, in turn, affect their behavior in organizational settings.

[1] David Easton, "The Perception of Authority and Political Change," in Friedrich, *op. cit.*, p. 185.

VARIATIONS IN DEFINITIONS
AMONG ORGANIZATIONS

After several introductory questions about organizational goals and individual job satisfaction, the members of the three organizations were asked to define authority in their own words (see Appendix for questions 5–5b). The definitions of authority advanced by the twenty-three policemen and the twenty members of the elementary school staff differed greatly. That differences in interpretation and nuance should occur was not surprising, but the abundance of dissimilar responses in all three organizations was certainly beyond expectation. Obviously, this was in part because of the unique personalities and experiences and hence unique perceptions of the people who were interviewed. Despite this uniqueness of personality and perception, it was hypothesized that the structure of authority characteristic of each agency would condition the ways in which authority was viewed.

Although all formal organizations of any complexity or permanence require an authority structure or network of hierarchical positions, the form that authority relations take may vary greatly from organization to organization. In Chapter II a number of variables crucial to the exercise of authority were emphasized. The organizations providing the field setting for this study were purposely selected to yield three differing environments, presumably varying in the degree to which members were allowed to participate in the making of critical decisions. It was expected that the militarylike hierarchy of the police department would emphasize formal authority based on position. In contrast, in the more permissive environment of the elementary school, it was expected that the principal and teachers would operate more as a collegiate body of equals with an emphasis on professional competence rather than formal rank. The welfare department was expected to fall somewhere between these extremes. As has already been indicated, the authority structure of the police department consisted of five distinct hierarchical ranks, the welfare office four, and the elementary school three. A further index of the differing emphasis on hierarchy was the ratio of supervisory personnel to rank-and-file workers, ranging from one to five in the police department, one to six in the welfare office, and one to seventeen in the elementary school.

The interview data presented in Table 4 tend to confirm these initial expectations about authority in the three agencies. Police department personnel, in particular, and welfare staff, to a considerable extent, expressed much greater interest in the internal authority structure of their respective organizations than did the teachers. However, a majority of the workers in all three organizations gave no explicit indication of their concern or expressed only a passive interest in internal authority relations. For example, a clerical worker replied: "As for authority, I don't care for it. It doesn't mean too much to me." On the other hand, police officers as a group and supervisory personnel in all three organizations were much more likely to express an active interest in authority. Thus, the top executive of one agency was keenly aware of the need for assessments of authority: "We've been wrestling with them [authority and responsibility] in job descriptions." Active interest was also expressed by a line supervisor who had "a very strong feeling that authority and responsibility could not be separated" and then detailed the reasons for this.

TABLE 4

SUPERIOR AND WORKER CONCERN WITH
INTERNAL AUTHORITY RELATIONS

	Police department		Welfare office		Elementary school	
	Superiors $N = 7$	Workers $N = 26$	Superiors $N = 4$	Workers $N = 19$	Superiors $N = 1$	Workers $N = 19$
High concern, active interest	57%	35%	100%	11%	100%	5%
Medium concern, some interest	43	12	0	26	0	5
Low concern, passive interest, or concern not explicit	0	53	0	63	0	90
Total	100%	100%	100%	100%	100%	100%

Despite considerable differences in the hierarchical structures and organizational environments, clear-cut organizational distinctions between the *definitions* of authority put forth by the members of the three organizations were difficult to draw. At least a fourth of the members in each organization defined authority, not in abstract terms, but by singling out the name or rank of the person above them in the hierarchy. As would be expected, members of the police department in particular and supervisory personnel even more so than rank-and-file police officers were inclined to define authority in terms of the person in command or by identifying specific ranks or names, for example:

> Authority? I imagine that's somebody who's got the authority—the sergeant, the lieutenant, the chief—the authority to command.

> Well, authority, in my estimation, that would be someone who is in command. . . . Authority, like the chief or the lieutenant. Is that what you mean?

In part, this tendency to define authority in terms of formal positions may be the result of the emphasis placed on "worn-on-the-shoulder rank" in the military environment of the police department. The relative infrequency of abstract, dictionary meanings could also be explained in part by the lower level of formal education characteristic of police department personnel.

Other definitions offered by the members of these three organizations ranged from one- or two-word equivalents, such as "authority is control" or "authority is respect," to more elaborate definitions which referred to authority as a capacity or ability to do certain things or to make certain decisions. The following responses by a social worker and a schoolteacher illustrate this category:

> Authority is . . . someone in authority, is someone with the power to control things, to make decisions and plans and see that they are followed through.

> He who has the authority has the power, although he doesn't necessarily exercise that authority, to control the actions of those on a level below him.

Schoolteachers were more likely to define authority in terms of expertness or knowledge, for example:

> Authority? You mean as a person? . . . Authority is a source, a source of tested information, experience and ideas —would you read that back to me—by those regarded as educated individuals in a certain area.

> Authority? Authority to me, more or less, is someone that knows what it is all about and knows how to do it. He has the knowledge, and he can express it.

A final category of definitions was so divergent as to almost defy classification. These definitions ranged from the interpretation which saw authority as "the one to whom you pass the buck" to "setting an example, morally and ethically."

DISTINCTIONS BETWEEN SUPERIORS AND WORKERS

A basic hypothesis of this study was that level in the hierarchy would be one of the crucial determinants of perceptions of authority. Not only would supervisory personnel express a more active concern with internal authority, but they would also tend to regard it in more positive terms than their subordinates (see Table 4). Variations in definitions of authority among superiors as contrasted with workers did occur. In general, supervisory personnel were inclined to define authority as an attribute of position, such as the capacity to give orders or make rules. Rank-and-file members were more likely to put forth neutral definitions, such as expertise, which tended to minimize or play down unequal positions in the hierarchy. These differences with regard to definitions of authority must be interpreted with considerable caution, however, because of the heterogeneity of responses and the limited number of cases. This is particularly true of the elementary school, where only the principal held supervisory rank.

One of the fundamental distinctions between the perceptions of authority held by supervisory personnel and those held by rank-and-file workers is differing emphasis on internal and external authority relationships. This study concentrated on *internal* authority relations—those taking place between superior and subordinate employees of the organization—rather than *external* authority relations—those taking place between officials and clientele.[2] In addition to internal working relationships, governmental employees are confronted with a complex interdependency which includes both a responsibility to and an authority over citizens. The welfare worker, police officer, and schoolteacher are on the one hand "public servants" and on the other hand wielders of strong sanctions over their clientele: citizens in general and welfare recipients, law violators, and pupils in particular.

Despite the phrasing of the question which was oriented toward internal authority relations, a substantial minority of the members of each organization, when asked to define authority, clearly distinguished between their interactions with superiors and their contacts with clientele. A third to one-half of the personnel in each organization voluntarily advanced this distinction. For example, when asked, "What does authority mean to you?" a police officer replied, "Do you mean my authority as a police officer or my superior officer's authority over me?" Frequently, the distinction between external and internal authority came only after the respondents were asked to assess their own authority in comparison with other positions in the organization. For example, the following distinction was made by a young schoolteacher: "Well, I have complete authority over my classroom. I don't have any authority as far as the rest of the school."

As Table 5 indicates, superiors tended to perceive authority in

[2] As Chester I. Barnard and others have noted, organizations can be defined either "tightly" or "loosely," depending on whether one limits the analysis to the consciously coordinated activities of management and employees or extends the definition of organization to encompass investors, suppliers, distributors, customers, and clientele. In the legal and formal sense the latter participants are not members of the organization, but in the behavioral sense they are, even though not directly subject to the internal hierarchy of authority. Barnard, *Organization and Management, op. cit.,* pp. 112–125; March and Simon, *op. cit.,* pp. 89–90; James D. Thompson and Arthur Tuden, "Strategies, Structures and Processes of Organizational Decision," in James D. Thompson *et al.,* eds., *Comparative Studies in Administration* (Pittsburgh: University of Pittsburgh Press, 1959), p. 210.

terms of internal authority relationships alone; their subordinates, on the other hand, were more likely to define authority in both its internal and external dimensions. Although the elementary school principal could be considered an exception to this general pattern, even he discussed authority almost exclusively in terms of his relations with the superintendent and the teachers, mentioning his concern with children and parents only in passing.

TABLE 5

PERCEPTIONS OF SUPERVISORY PERSONNEL AND WORKERS AS TO INTERNAL AND EXTERNAL AUTHORITY RELATIONS

	Police department		Welfare office		Elementary school	
	Superiors $N=7$	Workers $N=26$	Superiors $N=4$	Workers $N=19$	Superiors $N=1$	Workers $N=19$
Internal authority relations only	86%	42%	75%	37%	0%	42%
Both internal and external relations	14	50	25	52	100	47
External authority relations only	0	8	0	11	0	11
Total	100%	100%	100%	100%	100%	100%

A number of plausible explanations for this pattern could be suggested. First, rank-and-file workers are in continual daily contact with clientele whereas the supervisory personnel are brought in only on the more complex cases. As one social worker put this point, "The people who are higher up have become further removed from the job—they see things in a different light." Furthermore, supervisory personnel are probably more conscious of internal authority because of its usefulness as a mechanism for coordination and control, in addition to the possible personal gratification that such authority may provide. Subordinates, on the other hand, tend to minimize the importance of internal authority, perhaps for opposite reasons.

THREE VIEWS OF AUTHORITY

Perceptions of authority depend on the unique personality and experiences of the participants in the authority relationship, the kind of organization in which these relationships take place, and the level in the hierarchy from which authority is viewed. This study has focused on the last two variables as they affect perceptions of authority. With one exception, all superiors and all subordinates were interviewed in organizations which were purposely selected to provide a range of behavior along the dimension of participation in the making of critical decisions. Although generalizations must be treated with considerable caution because these organizations may not be typical and because of the limited number of interviews, some conclusions can be advanced.

That differences in perceptions of authority should occur between police officers, welfare workers, and school teachers is hardly surprising. Despite their common culture and the fact that all three are local governmental subunits, each organization recruits a different kind of worker. Social workers and schoolteachers are predominantly women with college educations; police officers are men with little formal education beyond high school. The expected personality, behavior, and training which make for a good police officer are obviously very different from those demanded in a social worker or a teacher, and there are more subtle but important differences among the latter. Finally, these organizations were purposely selected to obtain variations in authority structure and hence variations in attitudes toward authority. In general, expected differences did occur as suggested in part by the evidence summarized in tables 4 and 5.

As would be expected, superiors in all three organizations expressed a higher concern with and took a more active interest in problems of authority. With the exception of a majority of the ranking officers in the police department, supervisors were more likely to define authority as an attribute of position or person, such as "the capacity to give directions" or "the person who makes decisions." The remaining ranking police officers and at least one-fourth of the members of all three organizations did not resort to abstract definitions or such equivalent terms as "power" and "control," but referred specifically to the name or the rank of their immediate superior: "Mr. Jones is the authority," or "The supervisor has the authority."

Another characteristic in which superiors differed from subordinates was their tendency to view authority strictly in terms of their relationships with employees. On the other hand, the subordinates of all three agencies were more likely to emphasize their relationships with clientele when asked to elaborate on the meaning of authority. That is, superiors emphasized internal authority relations; subordinates called attention to external authority relationships.

These differing views between superiors and subordinates suggest an important modification of Chester I. Barnard's seminal definition of authority as "the character of a communication (order) in a formal organization by virtue of which it is accepted." Barnard emphasized two aspects of authority: the subjective and the objective.[3] A revised definition should include a third aspect: the perspective of people in authority or those who issue the instructions or orders. This aspect is similar to Barnard's subjective aspect in that it, too, is personal. However, it focuses on the *superior's* attitudes and behavior—the initiation of orders with the idea that they will be accepted—rather than the subordinate's perceptions and actions—the accepting of the communication as authoritative. This point of view is implicit in the traditional administrative notion of authority conceived as an attribute of office which is projected on to orders passing from the superior down the "chain of command" to the subordinate. Under this revised conception, authority relations can be examined from at least three points of view: (1) the perceptions of the superior, (2) the perceptions of the subordinate, and (3) the perceptions of the observer of organizational behavior who orients himself not only to these perceptions but also views authority impersonally in terms of its impact on the achievement of organizational goals.

Of course, in any given organizational setting, these simplified notions are complicated by the fact that, with the exception of the

[3] *The Functions* . . . , *op. cit.*, p. 163.

lowest echelon, all members of the organization are involved in a series of overlapping authority relationships. Each individual is subordinate to a few, coordinate with some, and perhaps superior to others. The dilemma of the line foreman is well known, although less research has focused on similar conflicts in allegiance which confront middle management. Another way of describing this dilemma is to refer to multiple and overlapping responsibilities: to one's self, one's peers, one's superiors and subordinates, to the organization as a whole, and to the public at large.

RESPONSIBILITY AND AUTHORITY

The concept of responsibility has perhaps been surpassed in its general vagueness and differing usages only by words like "authority" and "power." Although the focus has been different, responsibility, like authority, has been a central concern of students of both public and private administration.[4] To begin to treat this concept adequately would require analysis and empirical inquiry as directed and lengthy as this study of authority. Hence, this examination of responsibility will be restricted to a number of brief comments on the meaning of the concept, together with a brief summary of the responses to several questions in the interview schedule oriented toward the term (see Appendix for questions 6–6b). These questions were included in the interviews because of the frequent association of authority and responsibility in the traditional literature of management. In common with other "principles of administration" in vogue during the 1930's and 1940's, this principle is more prescriptive than descriptive.[5] The link takes the form of an admonition to

[4] Four examples of recent attempts at clarification of the concept and ordering of the literature are: Glendon A. Schubert, Jr., " 'The Public Interest' in Administrative Decision-Making," *American Political Science Review*, LI (1957), 346–368; Arch Dotson, "Fundamental Approaches to Administrative Responsibility," *Western Political Quarterly*, X (1957), 701–727; Charles E. Gilbert, "The Framework of Administrative Responsibility," *The Journal of Politics*, XXI (1959), 373–407; and Carl J. Friedrich, ed., *Responsibility* (New York: Liberal Arts Press, 1960). For a contribution focusing on responsibility in the internal managerial sense, see Elliot Jaques, *The Measurement of Responsibility* (Cambridge: Harvard University Press, 1956).

[5] For a review of the "principles" literature, see Waldo, *The Adminis-*

managers that the delegation of responsibility should be accompanied by a "commensurate" delegation of authority or vice versa. Three such "enduring guideposts of organization" have been conveniently brought together and quoted with approval in John Millet's commentary on the working concepts of organization. This essay was written just after World War II and appeared as one of a collection of essays by leading students of public administration.[6]

> Responsibility should always be coupled with corresponding authority.[7]

> Authority must be commensurate with responsibility.[8]

> Responsibility must be accompanied by reasonably complete authority.[9]

Before commenting further on the "principle" that "authority should be commensurate with responsibility," it is necessary (1) to briefly distinguish between two kinds of responsibility, one of which seems to merge into the other, and (2) to specify differences between authority and responsibility. Both kinds of responsibility refer to attributes of a relationship between two persons or groups in which one acts for or in the name of the other. However, one kind of responsibility, which, for want of a better classification, can be referred to as internal responsibility, occurs in organizations as narrowly defined. This is the kind of responsibility dealt with in such administrative maxims as the above. The second kind, external

---

trative State, op. cit., pp. 162–191. See also Simon, *Administrative Behavior, op. cit.,* pp. 20–44. Simon's trenchant criticism was first published as "The Proverbs of Administration," *Public Administration Review,* VI (1946), 53–67.

[6] Fritz Morstein-Marx, ed., *The Elements of Public Administration* (Englewood Cliffs, N.J.: Prentice-Hall, Inc., 1946), pp. 140–157. Suggestive of the general abandonment of the search for enduring *principles,* this was one of the few articles which was completely revised for the second edition (1959) of this work.

[7] "Ten Commandments of Good Organization," prepared by the American Management Association and quoted in *Public Administration Review,* III (1943), 80, n. 1.

[8] Donald C. Stone, *The Management of Municipal Public Works* (Chicago: Public Administration Service, 1939), p. 7.

[9] W. R. Allsetter, "Comments on the 'Ten Commandments,'" *Public Administration Review,* III (1943), 81.

responsibility, generally refers to relationships between public servants and citizens. In other words, how do citizens ensure that government, particularly the bureaucracy, is responsive to the public interest? One of the difficulties of the concept of responsibility is that it can be used both descriptively and normatively and the use intended is not always made clear. The focus in the discussion to follow is mainly on internal responsibility, a responsibility seen from the perspective of the incumbents of formal positions in the hierarchy vis-à-vis their superiors, equals, and subordinates. The problem of external responsibility, which also includes the relationships of administrative agencies to higher executives and the legislature and courts, must remain a peripheral concern. It should be noted, however, that organizational members will sometimes mention external responsibilities, for example, obligations to the public or the community at large, as grounds for ignoring or disobeying responsibilities to the organization, their fellow workers, or their superiors.

Superior-subordinate relationships in organizations are characterized by attributes of both authority and responsibility. Authority refers to the range of activities which a superior can order a subordinate to perform with high expectations that he will carry these *activities* out. Responsibility also carries with it a specification of range, but this specification is in terms of the *goals* of the organization. A superior has responsibility for the achievement of a given set of goals and authority over a given set of activities.[10] He may delegate authority over the activity to subordinates, but he still maintains responsibility. This "paradox of delegation" and the inadequacy of a principle advocating that "authority correspond to responsibility" receive extensive comment from Chester I. Barnard in his review of Charles S. Hyneman's book, *Bureaucracy in a Democracy*.[11] Barnard takes Hyneman and the traditional management literature to task for reiteration of the principle without an examination of its implications. No matter how much lip service is paid to "authority commensurate with responsibility" as an ideal,

[10] James S. Coleman, "Systems of Social Exchange" (Department of Social Relations, The Johns Hopkins University, 1963), p. 22. (Mimeographed.)

[11] Review of Charles S. Hyneman's *Bureaucracy in a Democracy* in *American Political Science Review*, XLIV (1950), 990–1004.

the facts of administrative behavior are apt to be quite different.
As Barnard asserts:

> . . . Most of the work of formal organizations is accomplished
> under responsibility without authority, or in excess of author-
> ity, or without use of or reliance upon authority. Responsi-
> bility and authority are not unrelated, but that they are
> "commensurate" (assuming this can have meaning with re-
> spect to concepts, neither of them susceptible of objective
> measurement) is contrary to experience and observation.[12]

Furthermore, as Barnard convincingly argues, this frequent lack of
correspondence leads to something of a paradox as far as the delegation of authority and responsibility is concerned. The delegator does
not relieve himself of either authority or responsibility; in fact, he
increases both.

> The effect of delegation is to diminish (but not neces-
> sarily extinguish) the control (in the case of authority) and
> the responsibility for the *specific* case as distinguished from
> the *aggregate* of cases. The delegator divests himself of no
> responsibility for the aggregate result by delegating authority
> or by sharing restricted responsibility with others. Indeed, it
> is by either kind of delegation that he utilizes his authority
> or attempts to better discharge his responsibilities.[13]

That is, although authority and responsibility can be divided
in many ways, they are never diminished by delegation. A superior
can delegate authority for doing a job, but he still retains the responsibility for seeing that the job is done. This retention or increase
in responsibility, because of and not in spite of delegation, finds
confirmation in the remarks of one of the ranking officers in the
police department:

> As far as accountability and responsibility, I still have
> responsibility no matter how I delegate. The men under me
> are accountable for their jobs, but I'm responsible. My re-
> sponsibility is for carrying out my job. The chief doesn't
> come around and say, "Do this" or "Do that," but I'm ac-
> countable to him. The police officers under me are account-
> able to me. It's my responsibility to see that the job is carried
> out.

12 *Ibid.*, pp. 1001–1002.
13 *Loc. cit.*

The paradox of the delegation of authority and responsibility also has implications for decision-making theory. It suggests that, the more superiors decentralize decision-making, the more centralized and rigorous must be their auditing of decisions made by their subordinates.[14]

If this vague and oversimplified "principle"—that authority should be commensurate with responsibility—has any meaning at all, a further question needs to be asked: to *whom* is a person responsible and for *what?* If one asks the members of an organization this question, it soon becomes clear that responsibility is much more complex than this principle would have us believe. There is no single responsibility; rather, there are multiple responsibilities, and these responsibilities frequently overlap and conflict. A person's responsibility to himself may tell him to do one thing, his responsibility to his superior may dictate another option, his responsibility to his particular clientele may suggest a third possibility, and all three alternatives may be in violation of the existing rules and regulations set forth in administrative manuals.

The response of a schoolteacher illustrates the multiple responsibilities felt and expressed by the more articulate members of all three public service agencies:

> Everyone has some sort of responsibility. That's so broad. I have responsibility everywhere. I have responsibility at school, at home. . . . I suppose you mean mainly at school. I have a responsibility to the school district to try to teach what they have set up—their ideas and standards. I have a responsibility to my fellow teachers to maintain high professional standards in actual teaching and to maintain good personal relations. I have the same responsibility to the principal along these same lines . . . and a responsibility to the parents, and to the children, to be fair and consistent to each

[14] For extended comment on delegation, one of the most complex and least understood of managerial techniques, see Perrin Stryker, "The Subtleties of Delegation," *Fortune,* LI (1955), 94–97, 160–164. The trend toward centralized control under the impact of information technology is predicted in an article by H. J. Leavitt and T. L. Whisler, "Management in the 1980's," *Harvard Business Review,* XXXVI (1958), 41–48. See also Arnold S. Tannenbaum, "Control in Organizations: Individual Adjustment and Organizational Performance," *Administrative Science Quarterly,* VII (1962), 236–257.

> child, a responsibility to help each child find a place in so-
> ciety. Responsibility is like the age-old question, "What is
> your philosophy of education?" We're always kidding about it;
> it's hard to put into words.

This quotation also illustrates some of the broader categories of responsibilities, including those to self, fellow workers, superiors, governing boards, clientele, and the community and public at large.

About one-third of the workers in all three organizations express
a concern with responsibilities to self and to their fellow workers.
About three-fourths mention their responsibilities to their immediate
superiors or to the administration as a whole. Two-thirds of the
police officers and about half of the social workers and school personnel mention their responsibility to their job or specific duties. In
every organization, the proportion of ranking officers who express
an accountability to the elective board or the top external executive
is more than three to one as compared with rank-and-file workers.
Among lower-ranking subordinates, responsibility, like authority, is
generally viewed in terms of the immediate superior.

Instead of voicing a responsibility to the more abstract and indirect notions of professional standards or obligations to professional
organizations, many members expressed these standards more directly through references to services performed for their clientele.
The following excerpts from interviews with a welfare worker, a
police officer, and a schoolteacher illustrate this point:

> Responsibility? Well, it runs around authority a little bit.
> Ordinarily, you follow your responsibility as set down in the
> manual. You meet basic needs as far as the people are con-
> cerned and render any service as indicated. Rehabilitation as
> near as possible—working toward self-maintenance.

> Responsibility is, to me, an obligation to fulfill your job.
> This is something you're obligated to feel personally. When
> you accept the job, you accept certain responsibilities. . . .
> It gets greater as you go up in rank. The new patrolman, he
> accepts it when he puts the badge on his chest. He accepts an
> obligation or responsibility, whatever you call it. If it's a bum
> pinch, it's your responsibility to see that he makes a good one
> the next time. . . . With law enforcement, you're primarily
> responsible for life and property . . . the rights of all the

citizens. That's a big burden, really—constitutional rights. So many forget why we protect all citizens as such. . . .

In this situation here, of course, you have both your class and your administration to consider. On the classroom side, I feel responsible for the welfare of the class and providing a situation where they can learn. As far as the administration goes, I feel it my duty and responsibility to carry out the expressed view, the rules and regulations, and whatever they desire, that are set up by the administration.

Two-thirds of the welfare workers and schoolteachers emphasized responsibilities to clients as compared with only about one-fifth of the police officers. However, the latter's clientele is more diffuse, encompassing the entire public, and not so much a particular group such as welfare recipients or schoolchildren and parents. As one experienced police officer reports on this feeling of responsibility to the public at large:

Actually, being employed by the public, we're responsible to every citizen who pays taxes or lives within our jurisdiction. It's not like working for an employer where you're responsible to him alone. Here, it's everybody within your jurisdiction. And I'd go a little further. You're also responsible to your immediate supervisor—you can't foul him up. But, generally, to the public as a whole.

SUMMARY

Although Barnard warns of the difficulty of measuring authority and responsibility, if the desirability of balancing them is to be anything more than a trite saying echoed in administrative literature, these terms need further clarification through a number of empirical inquiries aimed at some form of measurements, however crude. Jaques' work with "the time-span of responsibility" as an objective measure of work level would seem to be a step in the right direction. The "time-span of responsibility" refers to the length of time an employee exercises discretion without being checked up on by a superior. As Jaques states the key problem:

This instrument required a specification of the following main points: how to discriminate between the discretionary content of the job and its nondiscretionary, or prescribed,

content; and how to determine the mechanisms by which a
manager reviewed his subordinate's use of discretion, and so
discretion on his own account.[15]

With some qualification, his comments are applicable to authority
as well. By way of contrast, most police officers have considerable
authority under the law, but limited discretion as to how the law
is to be applied. In general, however, the more discretion an official
has, the greater his authority.

[15] Jaques, *The Measurement* . . . , *op. cit.*, p. 33.

VI

Acceptance of Authority and the Implementation of Decisions

Why do some people in organizations accept the authority of others? Why is authority rejected? How does acceptance of authority facilitate the implementation of organizational decisions?

Authority relations are basic to understanding organizational decision-making because they constitute the primary structure within which organizational decisions are made and implemented. Furthermore, level of hierarchy is related to kind of decision-making. In general, the higher the level of hierarchy, the more prevalent innovative or nonprogramed decision-making will be.[1] At the risk of considerable oversimplification, organizational decision-making can be described as a two-stage process. First, there is the stage of *choice*. The decision-maker selects one alternative from among several

---

[1] March and Simon, *op. cit.*, pp. 139–140; Herbert A. Simon, "The Decision Maker as Innovator," in Sidney Mailick and Edward H. Van Ness, eds., *Concepts and Issues in Administrative Behavior* (Englewood Cliffs, N.J.: Prentice-Hall, Inc., 1962), pp. 66–69; William J. Gore, "Decision-Making Research: Some Prospects and Limitations," in *ibid.*, pp. 52–58.

limited alternatives which are available to him.[2] Second, there is the stage of *implementation*. Typically, this takes the form of spoken or written orders from superiors to subordinates. The subordinate who receives the order proceeds to carry it out or, in relatively rare cases, rejects the communication.

In practice, organizational decision-making is much more complex. The decision-maker is seldom isolated; a number of organizational members frequently participate in the choice stage of the decision-making process. Choice may include a decision to act or not to act, now or in the future. The decision, once made, may be communicated across and up, as well as down, the hierarchy from superior to subordinate. Omissions, alterations, and additions affect the communication.[3] Even in the most typical pattern, the subordinate has open to him a wide range of alternatives short of complete acceptance or rejection.

Furthermore, it should be noted that there is considerable play between choice and implementation, between preferred goals and the means to achieve these ends.[4] As William J. Gore suggests in one of the few comparative studies of decision-making in public agencies, administrators tend to react to decisions as whole events rather than perceive them as broken down into successive stages. They stress the continuing need for bargaining and negotiation not only within the agency, but also with external groups which can block or support the intended policy change.[5] Most of the literature

[2] "Choice is always exercised with respect to a limited, approximate, simplified 'model' of the real situation." March and Simon, *op. cit.*, p. 139. In that not all alternatives can be or are considered, policy-making is incremental rather than rational and comprehensive. See Charles E. Lindblom's imaginative development of an alternative model to rational choice, "the method of successive limited comparisons." "The Science of 'Muddling Through,'" *Public Administration Review*, XIX (1959), 79–88.

[3] William V. Haney, "Serial Communication of Information in Organizations," in Mailick and Van Ness, *op. cit.*, pp. 150–165.

[4] As Lindblom summarizes the interdependence of means and ends: ". . . Evaluation and empirical analysis are intertwined; that is, one chooses among values and among policies at one and the same time. Put a little more elaborately, one simultaneously chooses a policy to attain certain objectives and chooses the objectives themselves." "The Science . . . ," *op. cit.*, p. 82.

[5] William J. Gore, "Administrative Decision-Making in Federal Field Offices," *Public Administration Review*, XVI (1956), 281–291.

of decision-making concentrates on the theoretical clarification of the first stage—choice. There is little systematic empirical research treating of the second stage of decision-making—implementation. The many administrative case studies lead, at worst, to almost no generalizations and, at best, to a number of conflicting or contradictory hypotheses. Research findings from this study of authority relations may help to clarify how decisions are implemented in public organizations.

ACCEPTANCE AND REJECTION OF AUTHORITY

Two questions were devised to elicit recollection of instances of the acceptance and rejection of authority by the members of the welfare office, police department, and elementary school. The first question approached rejection of authority in a rather indirect manner, by asking each member whether he or she ever received instructions from above which seemed to conflict with his own views of what should be done (Question 7). The second question focused directly on the rejection of authority. Respondents were asked whether their superior had ever exercised his authority in a manner that was unacceptable to them (Question 8). After each question, members were asked to give either actual or hypothetical examples and to relate what they did or would do under the circumstances.

As already noted, it is possible for a "no" response to be interpreted in at least two contradictory ways. It might be that the superior has not in fact issued any incompatible instructions or exercised his authority in a manner unacceptable to the subordinate, or it could mean that the respondent hesitated to commit himself for fear that his dissatisfaction might get back to his superiors. By the time these questions were asked, about halfway through the interview, the rapport seemed to be sufficient to elicit fairly frank responses from all but two or three members in each of the three organizations.

Extent and Types of Rejection

As Table 6 indicates, the members of all three organizations recalled instances of conflict-producing instructions much more frequently than they reported experiences of their superior's unacceptable exercise of authority. Less than one-fifth of the members of the police department and welfare office indicated that they never received instructions from above which seemed to conflict with their own standards, whereas 40 per cent of the elementary school personnel reported no such instances. Acts of their superiors perceived as unacceptable exercises of authority were reported by 60 per cent of the membership of the welfare office as against 42 per cent and 35 per cent in the police department and elementary school, respectively. Several plausible interpretations of the differences between the three agencies may be advanced. It might be that the welfare office and police department were actually characterized by greater number of conflict-producing instructions and more arbitrary supervision than the elementary school. Welfare workers seemed generally more critical of their superiors. Police officers appeared more hesitant to discuss authority relationships for fear that criticisms might get back to their superiors. The schoolteachers apparently operated in a more independent atmosphere with less direct supervision, hence they received fewer instructions which seemed to conflict with their personal and professional standards. During periods of crisis or rapid growth, as organizational members were exposed to new problems for which precedents were lacking, instructions which aroused conflict might have been expected to increase.

"Yes" responses were also open to a variety of interpretations. First, there was the problem of evaluating the frequency of conflict-producing instructions or the arbitrary exercise of authority, a frequency which was not always determinable from the responses. Furthermore, a "yes" response was not only an indication of the extent of rejection of authority, but also reflected in part the member's willingness to discuss or criticize the existing authority structure. A subordinate might generally accept authority but still be critical of several instances when he or she felt that authority was unjustly exercised. When people report many instances of the unacceptable exercise of authority or the issuance of instructions bringing about conflict, however, they are undoubtedly closer to the threshold of complete rejection than a person who can recall only one or two instances.

The types of conflict-producing instructions received from

TABLE 6

PERCEPTIONS OF THE EXTENT OF CONFLICT-PRODUCING INSTRUCTIONS AND THE UNACCEPTABLE EXERCISE OF AUTHORITY

	Police department $N = 33$		Welfare office $N = 23$		Elementary school $N = 20$	
	Extent of conflict-producing instructions	Extent of unacceptable exercise of authority	Extent of conflict-producing instructions	Extent of unacceptable exercise of authority	Extent of conflict-producing instructions	Extent of unacceptable exercise of authority
Yes, frequently, or many times	12%	6%	27%	13%	0%	0%
Yes, on occasion, sometimes	24	3	17	13	5	0
Yes, infrequently, or one time	18	3	17	17	20	10
Yes, frequency not determinable	28	30	22	17	35	25
Yes	82%	42%	83%	60%	60%	35%
No or never has happened	18%	58%	17%	40%	40%	65%
Total	100%	100%	100%	100%	100%	100%

above ranged from disagreements over organizational policy and the procedures used to implement that policy, to misinformation, the demanding of extra and unnecessary tasks, and poor communication between the central offices and the suborganizations under study. Disagreements over procedural implementation of policies aroused the most complaints. About half of the welfare office and police department members and a third of the elementary school members provided illustrations of communications at variance with their own views. More concretely, social workers might disagree with the regulations for processing welfare grants, patrolmen might complain about special orders which restricted their enforcement of maximum speed laws, or teachers would take issue with central office suggestions as to scheduling of social studies or language classes.

The exercise of authority by superiors perceived as unacceptable by subordinates ranged from the supervisor's general manner or attitude and specific instances of arbitrary action or abuse, on the one hand, to failures to provide support or take action and too much leniency, on the other hand. Disagreements over general policy and the procedures for carrying out policy also characterized conduct perceived as unacceptable. No clear-cut patterns emerged in any agency; rather, the types of unacceptable exercise of authority were fairly evenly distributed over the three agencies with somewhat more examples provided in the welfare office than either the police department or the elementary school.

The members were also asked what they did in response to conflict-producing instructions or the unacceptable exercise of authority. Tables 7 and 8 report typical reactions, which range from a conscious questioning but acceptance of the order as binding, to outright rejection or, as a last resort, transfer or resignation. The great majority of the members, from 60 to 91 per cent, would most characteristically take one of the first three types of reaction: (1) they would question the communication or order but carry it out anyway; (2) they would inform their superior of their views but seek to be converted; or (3) they would discuss the issue with their superior and work for change. From the short-range point of view, acceptance rather than rejection would seem to characterize most organizational activity. As one of the welfare department members described her relationship with her superior:

> She loves authority. I don't know why, and I don't try to figure it out. I just give it to her. It's just a trait she has. Her and I get along swell. No matter who is in authority, there's going to be resentment . . . usually from the most immature ones. I use to be that way, but not any more. If she wants me to stand on my head, I will.

TABLE 7

TYPICAL REACTIONS TO CONFLICT-PRODUCING INSTRUCTIONS

Reactions	Police department $N = 33$	Welfare office $N = 23$	Elementary school $N = 20$
Consciously questions but accepts as binding	64%	26%	30%
Informs immediate superior of views but complies or seeks to be converted	12	17	25
Discusses with immediate superior and works for change but still complies	15	39	5
Discusses but resists (evasion or modification despite seeming compliance)	3	0	0
Ignores, evades, or modifies without discussion	3	0	10
Discusses with, attempts to gain support by appeal to co-workers	3	9	15
Goes over superior's head, brings in other rank, seeks outside support	0	0	10
Open rejection	0	4	0
Transfer or resignation	0	0	0
No answer, no course of action given	0	5	5
Total	100%	100%	100%

TABLE 8

TYPICAL REACTIONS TO THE
UNACCEPTABLE EXERCISE OF AUTHORITY

Reactions	Police department $N = 33$	Welfare office $N = 23$	Elementary school $N = 20$
Consciously questions but accepts as binding	45%	43%	15%
Informs immediate superior of views but complies or seeks to be converted	12	17	35
Discusses with immediate superior and works for change but still complies	18	22	15
Discusses but resists (evasion or modification despite seeming compliance)	0	4	0
Ignores, evades, or modifies without discussion	3	4	0
Discusses with, attempts to gain support by appeal to coworkers	0	0	0
Goes over superior's head, brings in other rank, seeks outside support	0	0	5
Open rejection	3	0	0
Transfer or resignation	0	0	0
No answer, no course of action given	19	10	30
Total	100%	100%	100%

Police officers were more inclined to accept orders as binding without discussing them than either welfare workers or school personnel. One police officer put this point rather humorously:

> POLICE OFFICER: I've never had a superior say: "This is it; do it because I say to do it." They usually explain it to you, make you see the light, which I think is one of the better points of this department. But so far, none of the sergeants have said, "Do it."

INTERVIEWER: What if they did?

POLICE OFFICER: I'd do it. If someone should say, "I'm a sergeant, and I say so, period," I'd do it. Unless it was way out of line. If they said, "Jump off this bridge," I don't know whether I would. But as far as police matters go, they've been around here a lot longer than I have.

Other policemen, particularly patrolmen with more experience, would occasionally exercise more initiative when confronted with instructions from above which seemed at variance with their exercise of duty. For example, take the motorcycle patrolman's dilemma when confronted by a special order, issued by the chief of police, which governed the maximum speed allowable in the pursuit of speed law violators. This special order had been issued as a result of a traffic accident in a nearby city. Several innocent motorists had been killed when a speeding police car, in pursuit of delinquent teenagers, hit another vehicle at an intersection.

INTERVIEWER: Do you ever get instructions from above which seem to conflict with what you as patrolman feel you should do?

PATROLMAN: Well, yes. . . . There is an order governing maximum speed which we can use in pursuing a vehicle—50 miles per hour. . . . That's kind of stupid, but I'm in no position to argue with it. It comes right from the chief's orders. It's insubordination if you don't obey it, grounds for dismissal. It kind of puts you on the spot. . . .

INTERVIEWER: So what do you do?

PATROLMAN: I use my own discretion. I'll do 80 if I have to, and sometimes you do, knowing all the time, if I get caught by some city official, it may be grounds for dismissal. So far I haven't been nailed. But in order to get a vehicle going 50, you have to go faster than 50 to catch up. Otherwise you could follow it all the way across the nation.

INTERVIEWER: So how does this work out?

PATROLMAN: The general feeling is that it's just a club. If you happen to get in an accident, they could discharge you. I don't think they should do that. It kills whatever initiative you have. They should leave it to the officer's discretion. If there is a bank robbery and I'm in hot pursuit, I can follow orders and chase him at 50 miles per hour and get laughed out of the department. If I'm in hot pursuit and I hash up at 80 miles per hour, that's grounds for removal. You shouldn't have to be worried about this when you're doing the job—that's when you have the accident. You should be concentrating on the job itself.

They knew when they put it on we were going to violate it. You can't do an adequate job by obeying it. . . . Now it's direct violation of an order, whereas if they gave you more leeway, more discretion. . . .

When confronted with conflicting instructions or the unacceptable exercise of authority, schoolteachers were more likely to discuss these matters with their superiors and seek to be converted. The first reply is to the question on conflict-producing instructions; the second response is to the question on the unacceptable exercise of authority:

SCHOOLTEACHER A: First of all, I believe, if I were very concerned about it, I would tell him how I feel, and then I would go ahead and do it. If it were a minor thing, I'd tell [first name of principal] anyway, but I would go ahead and do what he wanted me to.

SCHOOLTEACHER B: No. . . . If he did, well, I'd tell him politely and very tactfully that I didn't agree. I'd try to talk things over with him and meet him halfway at least.

As Table 7 indicates, however, schoolteachers, when confronted by instructions from above which they disagreed with, were more likely to ignore the order, seek to gain support from their fellow workers, or even go over their superior's head and appeal to higher-ranking officials.

Welfare workers, in contrast, were inclined to discuss conflicting instructions or the unacceptable exercise of authority with their superiors and work for change. As one welfare worker reacted in response to conflicting instructions:

SOCIAL WORKER: Well, I think I would question it. I'd offer suggestions. And if I didn't think it was right, I'd offer suggestions and ask a question about it.

INTERVIEWER: Who would you ask?

SOCIAL WORKER: To my supervisor first and then, if we still have a question, to [district director]. First to the Grade I, and then to the Grade II, Supervisor and then the one above who made the suggestions.

The reaction of other welfare workers to conflicting orders might be to write a memorandum to the central office or to bring up the problem at a staff meeting.

In addition to the more typical responses summarized in tables 7 and 8, over half of the welfare workers and more than a third of the police officers and school personnel reported alternative reactions that they had taken or might take in response to what they perceived as unfair instructions or the arbitrary exercise of authority. These reactions ranged more widely and would more likely include subterfuge, evasion, or modification of orders without clearance. The following responses, one from a worker in each of the three organizations, illustrate these alternative behaviors:

POLICE OFFICER: Oh, there might be a different way you might want to do it. I wouldn't say it wasn't the right way. I might do it a little bit different my own way.

WELFARE WORKER: Sometimes she asks you to do things just because she knows you have to do it. But if you don't, there's very little that they can do. But usually you do it. Sometimes the things she asks us, they don't last very long, she's changeable. Sometimes you wait and see if she'll forget about it.

SCHOOLTEACHER: Well, if I were expected to carry out their ideas over mine, I suppose I'd carry them out. But I'd be reluctant. If I felt I'd get better results, I think I would stick with mine. I wouldn't resent them. If I felt their ideas were better than mine, I would give it a try anyway.

Other reactions might include seeking support from co-workers or going over the superior's head to make appeals to higher rank. For example, a clerical worker in the welfare department gave this response to the question about conflicting instructions:

Before, I would have gone in and talked to [Supervisor

X]. Now we go through channels. I clear with [Supervisor
Y], so she doesn't feel I'm doing something behind her back.
The minor ones we can work around.

A schoolteacher provided this illustration in response to the same
question:

> Well, I think I would treat it on a professional basis and
> talk to my colleagues, whether it was something different in
> this state or not. And if it wasn't, discuss it with them. Then
> I'd take it to the administration and, if I didn't get any satis-
> faction, go to the central office, or I would go to another
> principal, a friend of mine. I would air it with him. Or I
> could take it to the professional standards committee of our
> own teachers' association and from there to the state. [Pause]
> Well, it did occur, and that is the way I did it. . . .

Open rejection of an instruction or order was reported only
infrequently. Transfer or resignation from the organization was perceived as the last resort by some members. These reactions were
more likely to occur as a result of the unacceptable exercise of authority over a period of time. In rare instances transfers or dismissals
were initiated by superiors when subordinates failed to effectively
discharge responsibilities. Although no demotions or resignations
occurred during the field phase of this research, each organization
underwent a change in personnel as a result of a breakdown in
authority relations within a six-month period either before or after
this research was conducted. A sergeant had been reduced in rank
in the police department several months before this study began.
One of the supervisors in the welfare department was transferred to
the central office and demoted. A schoolteacher was transferred to
another school at the request of the principal.

What conclusions can be drawn from this summary of interviews with workers in three public service agencies? How does the
acceptance or rejection of authority affect the implementation of
organizational decisions?

SUMMARY

At first glance the acceptance of formal authority would appear to be a fairly simple phenomenon—a subordinate either car-

ries out decisions which have been made and communicated by his superior, or he does not. As the interview data from this study have demonstrated, acceptance of authority is much more complex. After reporting the extent and types of conflict-producing instructions and unacceptable exercises of authority as perceived by the seventy-six members of these three public service agencies, some of the more typical and extreme kinds of reactions were illustrated by specific excerpts from the interviews. Subordinates apparently found it easier to recall examples and discuss incompatible instructions than abuse of authority in all three organizations.

Acceptance of authority would seem to range along a continuum from a point where the subordinate exercises considerable initiative and carries out orders even before they are voiced to a shifting area of evasion and modification of orders just short of outright rejection at the other extreme. Between these two ends of the continuum, acceptance of authority ranges from situations in which decisions communicated from above are considered as advisory only, complied with despite a conscious questioning of their merits, or obeyed with indifference. It is only in this last or more restricted sense that, as Simon asserts, "A subordinate holds in abeyance his own critical faculties for choosing between alternatives and uses the formal criterion of the receipt of a command or signal as his basis for choice."[6] The range of alternative actions open to subordinates in organizational authority relationships is presented in Fig. 5.

This continuum also illustrates certain methodological problems encountered in observing authority relations in organizations. The same problems are encountered in categorizing responses to questions in which subordinates were asked how they reacted to conflicting instructions from above or their superior's unacceptable exercise of authority. When A asks B to carry out an order, B may respond in ways that cannot be classified simply as acceptance or rejection of authority. B may agree to act and then not act. This can be determined only by observation, preferably supplemented by follow-up interviews with both A and B. Or B may agree to act

[6] Simon, *Administrative Behavior, op. cit.,* pp. 126–127. Cf. Simon, Smithburg, and V. A. Thompson, *op. cit.,* p. 182.

and indeed carry out the order, but much later than A had in mind when he issued the order. Or B may act in response to A's order but actually do something quite different from what A proposed. This could result from a failure in communication caused by A's unclear instructions, B's lack of understanding, or both. Finally, B could do part of what A suggested but leave another part undone. All of these cases of misinterpretation, modification, or evasion fall somewhere between outright rejection and clear-cut acceptance of authority.[7]

Actual observation of the acceptance of authority is, of course, complicated still further by the frequent "invisibility" of the phenomenon. For, as Simon points out, "The more obedient the subordinate, the less tangible will be the evidences of authority."[8] Carl Friedrich refers to the same subtle process in a much broader context in his discussion of the rule of anticipated reactions:

> The influence of public opinion, or of parliament upon the conduct of governmental affairs is as devoid of ascertainable manifestations as the influence of a courtesan upon her royal master. Why should this be so? Because the person or group which is being influenced anticipates the reactions of him or those who exercise the influence.[9]

Thus, the subordinate carries out many "orders" from his superior without their ever being voiced. The superior can assume that many routine tasks will be accomplished without his ever having to initiate a formal order. T. D. Weldon is making much the same point when he observes that when people begin to ask, "Why should I obey A?" in tones other than theoretical, A has already lost, or is in the process of losing, his authority.[10]

For these reasons, the investigator may be diverted to instances of rejection of authority. The secretary breaks into tears and refuses

---

[7] This analysis paraphrases a similar methodological problem discussed by William F. Whyte dealing with the measurement of interaction in organizations. "An Interaction Approach to the Theory of Organization," in Haire, *op. cit.*, pp. 178–179.

[8] Simon, *Administrative Behavior, op. cit.*, p. 129.

[9] Friedrich, *Constitutional Government* . . . , *op. cit.*, p. 17.

[10] T. D. Weldon, *The Vocabulary of Politics* (Baltimore: Penguin Books, 1953), p. 56.

Fig. 5

Actions Open to Subordinates in Organizational Authority Relationships

Anticipation	Acceptance of authority		Modification and evasion		Rejection of authority
Orders anticipated and carried out*	Acceptance of orders without critical review	Conscious questioning but compliance‡	Discusses but works for changes	Ignores, evades, modifies orders	Appeals to co-workers or higher rank for support.
Exercise of initiative	Indifference†				Open defiance; resignation from organization

* Cf. Carl J. Friedrich's rule of anticipated reactions, *Constitutional Government and Politics* (New York: Harper & Bros., 1937), p. 17. Friedrich prefers the term "influence," rather than authority in this context.

† Cf. Barnard's zone of indifference, *The Functions . . .*, *op. cit.*, pp. 168–169.

‡ Simon's concept of the zone of acceptance appears to be broader than Barnard's zone of indifference. *Administrative Behavior*, *op. cit.*, pp. 133–134.

to make the corrections that her boss has demanded. The clerical worker seeks support from social workers when she disagrees with her supervisor's instructions. The police officer quits the force rather than submit to the "unfair" demands of his sergeant. Although this study focuses mainly on acceptance of authority, the examination of the polar or opposite phenomenon, rejection of authority, has helped to clarify the former. Instances of rejection of authority are more intense, less submerged, and thus may be more easily identified and recalled by participants in the authority relationship. The situation is somewhat analogous to the clinical psychologist focusing on abnormal or pathological cases rather than normal behavior and students of international relations concentrating on conflict rather than order or peaceful agreements among nations.

VII

The Bases of Authority:
Legitimacy, Position, Competence, and Person

Although authority is initially based on formal position, legitimacy, and the sanctions inherent in office, its acceptance is conditioned by several additional factors.[1] In analyzing such related phenomena as professional competence, experience, and leadership, which modify and condition the exercise of formal authority, several approaches can be taken. As was suggested in Chapter I, many social scientists prefer a clear distinction between authority, power, influence, and leadership, reserving the label "authority" for hierarchical status relationships between incumbents of formal positions in organizations.[2] In Chapter II, however, a review of the literature pointed

[1] Reprinted in part from Robert L. Peabody, "Perceptions of Organizational Authority: A Comparative Analysis," *Administrative Science Quarterly*, VI (1962), 463–482, with the permission of the editor of *Administrative Science Quarterly*.

[2] See, for example, Bierstedt, in Berger, Abel, and Page, *op. cit.*, pp. 67–81. In an earlier paper, Bierstedt defined authority as "institutional power," which appears to be a concept of authority somewhat broader than formal status relationships. "An Analysis . . . ," *op. cit.*, 736.

117

up an alternative approach. Other students of administration, notably Herbert A. Simon and Robert V. Presthus, would broaden the meaning of authority to include additional bases beyond formal position and the sanctions inherent in office.[3] Usage of the word and much of the interview data of this inquiry seem to support the more inclusive interpretations of Simon and Presthus. However, the development of a science of administration may necessitate either a restriction of the term "authority" to a more precise technical meaning or an abandonment of the term for purposes of rigorous theory-building. Which of these two uses of the term is finally adopted is not so important as making clear the implications of each. The bases of *formal* authority—legitimacy, position, and the sanctions inherent in office—need to be distinguished from the sources of *functional* authority, most notably, professional competence, experience, and human-relations skills, which support or compete with formal authority.

As will be argued below, in general, functional authority supports formal authority. In a given superior-subordinate relationship, it is the superior's lack of functional authority or the subordinate's possession of greater competence, experience, or personal skill which tends to undermine formal authority. Competition may also occur between incumbents of equal formal rank, but of different task or specialist orientations, as, for example, between the controller and the merchandise manager of a department store. Finally, competition between functional and formal authority may occur where hierarchical channels are ambiguous, a condition frequently characteristic of staff-line relationships.[4]

Before summarizing some empirical findings from this study, it may be useful to briefly review the writings of five prominent contributors to the study of authority relations in organizations—Max

[3] Simon, "Authority," in Arensberg *et al., op. cit.,* pp. 104–106; Simon, Smithburg, and V. A. Thompson, *op. cit.,* pp. 189–201; Presthus, "Authority in Organizations," *op. cit.,* 86–91.

[4] Cf. Victor A. Thompson's distinction between hierarchical and non-hierarchical authority, "Hierarchy, Specialization, and Organizational Conflict," *Administrative Science Quarterly,* V (1961), 499. See also Dalton, *op. cit.,* 342–351; Robert T. Golembiewski, "Toward the New Organization Theories: Some Notes on 'Staff,'" *Midwest Journal of Political Science,* V (1961), 237–259.

Weber, Lyndall F. Urwick, Herbert A. Simon, Warren G. Bennis, and Robert V. Presthus. Their contributions illustrate a growing consensus as to the importance of several bases of authority which condition its acceptance. Not all these social scientists have emphasized the same sources of authority, and they have frequently used different words to convey similar meanings, but the essential points of agreement can be classified under four broad categories: (1) authority of legitimacy; (2) authority of position, including the sanctions inherent in position; (3) authority of competence, including both technical skill and experience; and (4) authority of person, including leadership and human-relations skills (see Table 9).

AUTHORITY OF LEGITIMACY

Unlike the related concepts of power and influence, the concept of authority has implicit in it the notion of legitimacy. Philosophers have long struggled with the complex and continuing problems of political authority, couched in the language of theories of social contract and doctrines of political obligation. The employment relationship, evolving out of the relationship between master and servant, has frequently been phrased in the same language. Those in authority have the *right* to demand obedience; those subject to authority have the *duty* to obey.[5] Max Weber, whose influence permeates almost all studies of bureaucracy, classifies the types of authority "according to the kind of claim to legitimacy typically made by each."[6] Although both traditional authority and charismatic authority are owed to a *person*—the chief, or charismatic leader—"in the case of legal authority, obedience is owed to the legally established impersonal order."[7] As Talcott Parsons and Alvin Gouldner have pointed out, Weber sets forth but does not elaborate on several additional bases of legal-rational authority, for example, hierarchical office and technical knowledge and experience.[8] Other writers, most notably Simon and Presthus, have further developed these concepts

[5] Simon, Smithburg, and V. A. Thompson, *op. cit.*, pp. 189–201.
[6] *The Theory . . . , op. cit.*, p. 325.
[7] *Ibid.*, p. 328.
[8] *Ibid.*, pp. 58–60, n. 4; Gouldner, "Organizational Analysis," in Robert K. Merton, Leonard Broom, and Leonard S. Cottrell, Jr., eds., *Sociology Today* (New York: Basic Books, 1959), pp. 400–423.

TABLE 9
THE BASES OF AUTHORITY

	Formal authority		Functional authority	
	Legitimacy	Position	Competence	Person
Weber*		Legal-rational authority		Traditional authority
	Legal order	Hierarchical office	Technical knowledge, experience	Charismatic authority
Urwick†		Formal, conferred by the organization	Technical, implicit in special knowledge or skill	Personal, conferred by seniority or popularity
Simon‡	Authority of legitimacy, social approval	Authority of sanctions	Authority of confidence (technical competence)	Techniques of persuasion (as distinct from authority)
Bennis§		Role incumbency	Knowledge of performance criteria	Knowledge of the human aspect of administration
Presthus‖	Generalized deference toward authority	Formal role or position	Technical expertise	Rapport with subordinates, ability to mediate individual needs

* Weber, *The Theory* . . . , *op. cit.*, pp. 328, 339.
† Urwick, *The Elements* . . . , *op. cit.*, p. 42.
‡ Simon, in Arensberg *et al.*, *op. cit.*, pp. 104–106; Simon, Smithburg, and V. A. Thompson, *op. cit.*, pp. 189–201.
§ Bennis, *op. cit.*, 288–289.
‖ Presthus, "Authority in Organizations," *op. cit.*, pp. 89–91.

of the underlying bases of authority. Although Simon uses "authority of legitimacy" in the narrower sense utilized here, Presthus extends the concept of "legitimation" to include all processes by which authority is accepted, reserving the concept of a "generalized deference to authority" (which, in turn, reflects the process of individual socialization) for this narrower sense of ethical sanctification.[9] For Simon, it is through the indirect mechanism of social approval from the particular reference group that the motive of legitimacy obtains its greatest force.[10] But whether used in the broad or narrow sense, authority of legitimacy is inextricably fused in reality with a second source or base frequently discussed in the literature—authority of position.

AUTHORITY OF POSITION

Robert K. Merton restates Weber's classic treatment of authority based on hierarchical office: "Authority, the power of control which derives from an acknowledged status, inheres in the office and not in the particular person who performs the official role."[11] That is, when a person becomes a member of an organization, he is already predisposed to accept orders given to him by persons acknowledged to be his superiors by their position in the formal organizational chart.

> In joining the organization [the employee] accepts an authority relation; i.e., he agrees that within some limits (defined both explicitly and implicitly by the terms of his employment contract) he will accept as the premises of his behavior orders and instructions supplied to him by the organization.[12]

Although their language has been different, such writers as Urwick, Bennis, and Presthus all have referred to much the same thing when they discussed formal authority, role incumbency, and formal position.

Simon, among others, has given the authority of position an extended interpretation in his discussion of the authority of rewards and sanctions inherent in office. His assertions that "the most important sanctions of managers over workers in industrial organizations are (a) power to hire and fire, (b) power to promote and demote, and (c) incentive rewards," are equally true of public

---

[9] "Authority in Organizations," *op. cit.*, p. 88, n. 8.

[10] Arensberg *et al., op. cit.*, p. 106.

[11] *Social Theory and Social Structure* (rev. ed.; Glencoe, Ill.: Free Press, 1957), p. 195.

[12] March and Simon, *op. cit.*, p. 90.

organizations.[13] Both participants in a superior-subordinate relationship are aware of the disparities in sanctions which support the relationship. However, although the subordinate is subject to the commands of the superior, the superior depends on the subordinate to get the job done. The supervisor engages in periodic ratings of his workers, ratings which affect promotion, pay raises, and even the chances of keeping the job. But if subordinates take no initiative, solve no problems for themselves, do everything the superior asks them but *no more*, the superior will soon be faced with the impossible task of trying to do every job in the organization by himself.[14] On the other hand, as long as subordinates know that a superior controls ultimate sanctions to compel obedience if his orders are resisted, authority cannot be defined solely in terms of acceptance or consent.[15] But even this advantage possessed by the superior is not without its costs. As Peter M. Blau points out, the continued use, or threat of use, of sanctions will in the long run undermine authority. "This is the dilemma of bureaucratic authority; it rests on the power of sanction but is weakened by frequent resort to sanctions in operations."[16] One consequence of this mutual dependency with disparate sanctions is that the superior must broaden the base of his authority if he is to secure the active cooperation of his subordinates in achieving organizational goals. Formal authority flowing from legitimacy and organizational status must almost invariably be supported by authority based on professional competence and skill in human relations.

AUTHORITY OF COMPETENCE

Authority of competence is not limited to hierarchical relationships and, indeed, frequently cuts across the formal channels of communication. The new police sergeant seeks the advice of the veteran patrolman. Rather than consult with her superior, the older social worker calls a friend at the central office about the interpretation of a welfare department regulation. If, however, a superior

[13] Arensberg *et al., op. cit.,* p. 104.
[14] Leavitt, *op. cit.,* pp. 150–151.
[15] Presthus, "Toward a Theory . . . ," *op. cit.,* p. 57.
[16] *Bureaucracy in Modern Society, op. cit.,* pp. 76–77.

possesses both the appropriate technical skills and a wealth of experience, his formal authority is less likely to be challenged. In general, authority based on technical knowledge and authority based on experience are closely related, although distinctions can be made between them. Familiarity with certain operations can be gained only from day-to-day confrontation of problems. What may be a crisis for the beginner is routine to the old hand. Technical knowledge, in contrast with experience, is more likely to come from professional training, for example, specialized graduate education. Indeed, when promotional opportunities arise, seniority may frequently compete with technical proficiency; therefore the prerequisites for most supervisory positions stress both professional training and experience.

There remains, however, a more fundamental ambivalence regarding bases of authority in organizations. As Gouldner asserts, "One of the deepest tensions in modern organization, often expressed as a conflict between the line and staff groups, derives from the divergence of . . . two bases of authority"—authority legitimized by incumbency in office and authority based on professional competence.[17] Not only do subunits of organizations differ as to the importance attached to these two bases of authority, but different kinds of organizations in different times and cultures also seem to emphasize one or the other of these bases of authority.[18] Although a number of writers have commented on an increasing tendency toward reliance on professional competence with an attending decline in the perceived legitimacy of hierarchical authority, evidence suggests that the strategic location and influence of those in hierarchical

[17] Merton, Broom, and Cottrell, *op. cit.*, p. 414; see V. A. Thompson, "Hierarchy, Specialization . . . ," *op. cit.*, pp. 485–521, for an extended analysis of the conflict arising from growing inconsistencies between specialist and hierarchical roles.

[18] J. D. Thompson and Bates, *op. cit.*, pp. 332–334; Etzioni, "Authority Structure . . . ," *op. cit.*, pp. 43–67; Janowitz, "Changing Patterns . . . ," *op. cit.*, pp. 473–493; Bendix, *Work and Authority* . . . , *op. cit.;* Walter B. Miller, "Two Concepts of Authority," *American Anthropologist*, LVII (1955), 271–289; Stephen A. Richardson, "Organizational Contrasts on British and American Ships," *Administrative Science Quarterly*, I (1956), 189–207; Jaques, *The Changing Culture* . . . , *op. cit.*, p. 254; Hartmann, *op. cit.*, pp. 5–7.

roles often enable them to get along without specialized skills. Control of the organization's distribution system remains in hierarchical hands:

> Above what might be considered a market minimum, the satisfactions which the organization has to offer are distributed according to hierarchical rank. They include, in addition to money, deference, power, interesting activities and associations, conveniences, etc. Because these goods are distributed according to status rank, and access to any rank is controlled by . . . hierarchical position, these positions acquire great power. . . .[19]

The tension between authority of position and authority of competence, which appears to be endemic in hierarchical organizations, may sometimes be mediated by a fourth basis of authority, authority of person.

AUTHORITY OF PERSON

Authority based on legitimacy, position, and competence can be analytically distinguished from authority of person. Such a distinction takes a number of forms in the literature. As already suggested, Weber makes use of the distinction between authority based on office and authority based on personal attributes to differentiate the first of his three pure types of authority—legal-rational authority (itself containing seeds of other bases of authority) from his second and third types—traditional and charismatic authority.[20] Both Henri Fayol and Chester Barnard make similar distinctions between what Fayol referred to as "official authority" and "personal authority" and what Barnard described as "authority of position" and "authority of leadership."[21] A number of social scientists, including Bierstedt, Blau, Gibb, Selznick, and Urwick, have made analytical distinctions between authority and leadership.[22] The focus

[19] Victor A. Thompson, *Modern Organization* (New York: Alfred A. Knopf, 1961), p. 65.

[20] Weber, *The Theory* . . . , *op. cit.,* p. 328.

[21] Fayol, *General and Industrial Management,* trans. Constance Storrs (London: Pitman & Sons, 1949), pp. 19–21; Barnard, *The Functions* . . . , *op. cit.,* p. 173.

[22] Bierstedt, "The Problem of Authority," *op. cit.,* pp. 70–71; Blau, *The Dynamics of Bureaucracy, op. cit.,* p. 178; Gibb, in Lindzey, *op. cit.,* II,

in this study is not so much on personal or informal leader-follower relations, but rather on the *fusion* of leadership skills—be it charisma or routine human-relations skills—in a person who *also* occupies a position of authority; not on leadership as a personal quality, but on leadership as an organizational function.[23] Thus, as Bennis, Presthus, and others have suggested, "the knowledge of the human aspect of administration," "the ability to mediate individual needs," and a superior's leadership traits enhance the frequency and extent of acceptance of formal authority on the part of his subordinates.[24]

EMPIRICAL RESULTS

Although differentiating between authority of legitimacy, position, competence, and person facilitates understanding of complex organizational relations, do members of organizations also perceive these as important bases of authority?[25]

In response to the question, "What does authority mean to you?" all but about one-fifth of the members in each of the three organizations specified one or more sources from which authority came (see Appendix for complete wording of questions 5–5b). A summary of these reported bases of authority is presented in Table 10. The various sources of authority were classified according to the four analytical types developed from the literature. Despite the diversity of responses which was characteristic of all three organizations, the tendency to localize the source of authority in the top internal executive, immediate supervisor, or the worker's own position was particularly apparent. Representative excerpts from the interviews, some of which convey more than one source in a single response, illustrate the more specific classifications.

A number of members emphasized legitimacy or called more specific attention to legislation, manuals, or governmental institutions as bases of authority:

When I work any place, I feel that, whatever they want,

882; Philip Selznick, *Leadership in Administration* (Evanston, Ill.: Row, Peterson & Co., 1957), p. 24; Urwick, *Leadership* . . . , *op. cit.*, p. 37.

[23] Bavelas, *op. cit.*, p. 491.

[24] Bennis, *op. cit.*, pp. 283–287; Presthus, "Authority in Organizations," *op. cit.*, p. 91.

[25] Schutz, *op. cit.*, p. 267.

Table 10

Perceptions of the Bases of Authority in Three Public Service Organizations*

Bases of Authority	Police department N = 33	Welfare department N = 23	Elementary school N = 20
Authority of legitimacy			
Generalized legitimacy	12%	9%	10%
Law, state legislation, city ordinances, the state, county, city	15	17	15
Administrative codes, rules, regulations, manuals	0	17	0
Governing boards, policies of board	0	0	10
Authority of position			
Top *external* executive or executives, organization as a whole†	0	17	15
Top *internal* executive, ranking officers, administration as a whole‡	27	13	30
Immediate supervisor	9	39	0§
Inherent in position or job characteristics	30	26	15
Authority of competence			
Professional or technical competence, experience	15	22	45
Authority of person			
Personal characteristics or way in which authority is exercised	42	13	15
Other sources	6	4	0
No source specified	18	22	15

* Percentages total more than 100 per cent because some respondents indicated more than one base of authority.

† The category "top *external* executive" included the chief executives of the parent organizations, for example, the county manager, director of public welfare, city manager, and school superintendent.

‡ The category "top *internal* executive" included the police chief, the district director, and the principal.

§ Coded as "top *internal* executive" in the case of the elementary school.

> I give 'em. It's as simple as that whoever the boss is . . . [shrugs shoulders].

> Authority to me is something you're bound to obey. It's something that I respect.

> A lot of authority is in the manual—it's the law.

> Authority as far as I'm concerned is the rights we have as a policeman to do certain things. There is a certain authority given to us by the courts, by the state government. . . .

Several comments illustrate the many references to authority inherent in the position or in the people occupying certain ranking positions:

> The person with the rank has the final say. Whether you agree with him or not, you go along with him.

> My understanding of authority is that it is more-or-less part of a job, something which you have to accomplish, particularly as a supervisor or a director.

> Authority in reference to the ranking officers, the sergeants, the lieutenant, the chief? It's a sign or symbol to the average patrolman or average citizen that that man is in authority. He has—how would you put it?— . . . a little more power than the average patrolman within the police department.

> Authority is mostly our supervisor and grade-II supervisor.

Others emphasized professional competence or experience as the source of authority:

> I have the final word in licensing. There is no written law as to what a good foster home or what a bad foster home is except as we have defined it in our experience and knowledge. We have the authority to deny the license entirely. And it's based on this knowledge and experience rather than the manual.

> Well, my authority is completely within my classroom, and I'm given a great deal of authority there. And I'm appreciative of this. I'm given a complete rein. I can use my own philosophy, mainly because it's the philosophy of the district. With a good teacher, that's O.K. With a bad teacher, it's not.

The source of authority was also seen to depend on the way authority was exercised and on certain underlying personal traits:

> Authority in general? Oh, I don't know. I've never ob-jected to people having authority over me, if I felt they were competent. They don't have to be an intellectual or sharp looking, but they should at least be on an equal with me as far as mental and physical ability. If not, I'd object to it. I had some bosses back home, which I didn't go for. I still did the work. Maybe not as hard and not as efficiently, but I did it.

> Authority is based on someone to lead . . . so a person in authority would have to be a leader. He would have to have the ability to command and other traits of leadership. My favorite one is this: "They should back up their men." I hate a person who says out in front of everyone, "You did that wrong." He should stick up for his men.

Finally, authority might be seen as coming from other sources as mundane as a uniform—"Actually, I have no authority to the other men, but the police uniform gives you a certain authority out in the public"—or from such "ultimate" sources as the social worker who saw authority as "God given" or the police officer who ex-pressed the view that authority was derived from "the people as a whole."

In Table 10 we saw that authority of position was emphasized in the police department, particularly the authority delegated from the chief of police or incorporated in all ranking officers of the organization. In an organization where formal rank—epitomized by uniforms, insignia, and military courtesy—plays such an impor-tant part in day-to-day activity, it could hardly be otherwise. The amount of authority attributed to sergeants and inspectors (theoreti-cally of the same rank) varied extensively, but each of these officers was well aware that he had more formal authority than a patrolman, if less than the lieutenant or police chief. What was somewhat sur-prising, however, was the importance attached to authority of person. Not only was skill in human relations singled out more fre-quently than any other basis of authority, but police officers also placed much greater emphasis on such skills than did social workers or elementary-school teachers. In part, of course, this was a reflection of the type of activity that differentiates these jobs as well as the kind of person attracted to them. These findings also seem to support Janowitz's conclusions that in militarylike establishments skill in interpersonal relations rather than technical competency is emphasized as the basis of authority.[26] As younger, career-oriented police officers with college training in police administration replace older, "small-town cops," the importance attached to authority of competence in this police department will probably increase.

Another unexpected finding was the extent to which social workers, in contrast to police officers and elementary-school teachers, singled out authority of position. Approximately 40 per cent of the twenty-three members of the public welfare branch office mentioned their immediate supervisor as a source of authority. Authority inherent in their own position was the second most frequently mentioned basis of authority, followed by authority of competence (Table 10). In part, the social workers' emphasis on the authority of their immediate supervisor reflected the matriarchal role assumed by one of the three line supervisors, an older woman who had played an instrumental role in creating the branch office and who felt responsible for its entire operation. Workers who rejected her authority or served under other supervisors were more likely to mention the authority implicit in their jobs or to cite administrative manuals or regulations. The relatively low degree of importance attributed to authority of competence may have been a function of the lack of graduate professional training characteristic of all but three members of the staff.

Perhaps the most striking contrast between these three public service agencies was the relative importance attached to authority of professional competence in the elementary school. Almost half of the twenty-member school staff singled out this basis, compared with 22 per cent of the welfare workers and only 15 per cent of the police officers. This was in part related to the fact that 75 per cent of the school staff had had graduate training, including nine teachers with the equivalent of master's degrees or beyond. Furthermore, all school staff members except the secretary and the custodian belonged to two or more professional organizations, compared with

[26] "Changing Patterns . . . ," *op. cit.,* p. 492.

about half the members of the police department and about one-quarter of the welfare workers. Although the principal of this school played a more passive, democratic leadership role than either the police chief or the district director, his position or the school administration as a whole was the next most frequently mentioned source of authority in the school.

It was earlier suggested that functional authority based on technical and human-relations skills might serve to bolster formal authority based on legitimacy and position. In the course of these interviews with public service employees, however, numerous examples were cited which seem to suggest a basic ambivalence, if not an inherent conflict, between these bases of authority. Approximately 40 per cent of the members in each of the three organizations responded to a question on whether they ever received conflicting instructions from above with either a concrete example of authority of competence taking precedence over the authority of position or acknowledged the supremacy of authority based on technical skills in certain spheres of their work (see Appendix for complete wording of questions 7–7c). The following quotation from an interview with a veteran patrolman illustrates a situation in which authority based on technical knowledge supersedes a higher-ranking officer's authority of position:

> Last Tuesday a man came out of the bar with another man chasing him, carrying a rifle. He fired three shots and then left. The guy being shot at told us the story. I picked up a .22 short shell on the property. The [ranking officer] came out and said, "Make it up as a 417." That's displaying a weapon in a rude and unlawful manner. It's only a misdemeanor. It would have meant I couldn't have arrested him, and yet he fired three shots at somebody. That's assault with a deadly weapon at a minimum, a felony. They should throw the book at that guy! A misdemeanor? Ridiculous. And I told the [ranking officer] so. I finally got him to change it to my way, and finally, a day later, I did arrest the man.

A more typical reaction to conflicting instructions from above in the police department and the welfare office and, to a lesser extent, in the elementary school was, particularly among less-experienced members, acquiescence to authority of position.

SUMMARY

A survey of the bases of authority posited by five contributors to organizational theory—Weber, Urwick, Simon, Bennis, and Presthus—reveals considerable consensus, despite differing terminology. From writings of these and other social scientists, four analytical types of authority relations have been developed: (1) authority of legitimacy, (2) authority of position, (3) authority of competence, and (4) authority of person. This typology also seems to be useful for ordering perceptions of authority by seventy-six members of three public service agencies. Interactions between superiors and subordinates contain elements of all four types of authority, although the relative importance of each would seem to vary from person to person as well as from organization to organization. Over one-third of the members of all three organizations, particularly welfare department employees, emphasized legitimacy and position as important bases of authority. In addition, police officers stressed authority of person, whereas school employees emphasized authority of competence.

VIII

Organizational Authority: Conclusions

The principal objective of this study has been clarification of the concept of authority as a means of describing a central phenomenon of organizational behavior: authority relationships. For the most part an attempt to define authority in a single phrase or several sentences has been avoided. As Carl J. Friedrich has observed:

> Scientific defining must start from the phenomena, rather than from the words. Therefore, it is important to avoid asking what "authority" or something else of this order "really is" or "really means" (asking, in other words, for the essence of it), and to ask instead what the general features, traits or characteristics of a set of phenomena are, describe them in general terms and then attach to them the verbal symbol most nearly suitable among the available words.[1]

Given the exploratory nature of this study, my own preference has been to cast a large net rather than a small one. Although the primary focus has been on formal authority, an authority based on

[1] *Man and His Government* (New York: McGraw-Hill, 1963), p. 2.

legitimacy and position, this study has also dealt with such related phenomena as professional competence and leadership skills, here termed functional authority. Formal authority combined with functional authority generates "the actual power to get things done or to prevent their being done."[2]

It is now possible to bring together for elaboration five defining characteristics of organizational authority: its relational, hierarchical, organizational, temporal, and normative aspects.[3] These aspects are little more than arbitrary but convenient rubrics under which some of the most important properties and processes characteristic of organizational authority can be summarized.

One analytical distinction which all social scientists examining authority and such related concepts as power and influence have had to take into account, either implicitly or explicitly, is whether to treat these concepts as (1) a *property* or attribute of an individual or group or (2) as a *relation* between two or more individuals or groups. Thus, it is one thing to say, "A has authority," in much the same language as you would describe the color of his hair. It is something else to describe a relationship between individuals A and B in which the reciprocal attitudes and activities of each participant are taken into account. Although the difference may at first seem slight, it has considerable significance for the way in which authority is perceived and acted upon in concrete organizational settings and the manner in which the problem of authority is researched.

Although authority is occasionally discussed as if it were an attribute or property of an individual or office, particularly in the early literature of administration and bureaucracy, there is always

---

[2] Arnold Brecht, "How Bureaucracies Develop and Function," *Annals of the American Academy of Political and Social Science*, CCXCII (1954), 1.

[3] In his article comparing a contemporary European authority relationship with the absence of such a relationship in central Algonquin tribes in the seventeenth century, Walter B. Miller suggests six important analytical characteristics of the former: (1) the directive component, (2) role base, (3) permanence, (4) prestige differentials, (5) functional differentials, and (6) differential access to a system of rules. *Op. cit.*, pp. 275–276. Several of these characteristics are roughly comparable with the analytical dimensions independently developed here. His other characteristics have been subsumed under hierarchical and relational aspects of authority.

an implicit recognition that the person or office of authority has that authority vis-à-vis some other person or office. "The central idea in authority relations is that of the reciprocal control and reinforcement of behavior of two persons."[4] The notion of "reciprocal interdependence" needs qualification, however, for, while both members of the relationship depend on each other, it is not a relationship between equals.

These two ideas, taken in juxtaposition, shed considerable light on the dynamics of authority relationships. Although the link is mutual dependency, both participants are aware of the disparities in the sanctions which support the relationship. While the subordinate is subject to the commands of the superior, the superior depends on the subordinate to get the job done. Superior-subordinate roles may be characterized by their interdependency; they are also by definition hierarchical.

The second dimension of authority relations in organizations which needs emphasis is *hierarchy*. That is, authority relations take place between persons or positions of differing ranks. A common characteristic of all these relationships—superior-subordinate, expert-layman, master-servant, teacher-pupil, supervisor-worker—is that they are asymmetrical. This is true of all authority relations from the most visible vertical control in militarylike bureaucracies to the more subtle, but nevertheless pervasive, authority relations among professional staffs. This differing rank has multiple consequences in terms of job functions, the directions in which most orders and instructions flow, prestige, and the way authority is viewed. Each of these consequences which react upon one another and affect other dimensions of authority as well need brief elaboration.

The hierarchical nature of authority relations obviously affects as well as reflects task differentiation in the organization. This is only to say that superiors and their subordinates do different things. Little needs to be added to the existing commentaries on the implications of specialization and the division of labor. All that this means in the present context is that, while rank-and-file members execute the basic tasks of the organization—instructing and counsel-

    [4] J. S. Adams and A. K. Romney, "A Functional Analysis of Authority," *Psychological Review*, LXVI (1959), 234–251, 235.

ing students, providing services and financial assistance to welfare recipients, enforcing the laws and patrolling the streets—supervisors are responsible for directing and coordinating these activities.

Hierarchy not only implies an awareness of which position or person is superior and which is subordinate, but it also conveys a great deal of information about which way communications will flow, particularly instructions and orders as distinguished from reporting and informational messages. As Miller puts this, "The defining characteristic of this authority relationship is that by virtue of occupying a given position in a patterned role-relationship, one individual is empowered to direct the actions of another, and the other is obligated to accept that direction."[5] Furthermore, authority is transitive: if A has authority over B and B has authority over C, it follows that A also has authority over C.

In addition, the occupant of the superior position is accorded greater prestige than the occupant of the subordinate position. This difference is manifested in various ways—through deferential behavior, symbols of superior status, differences in compensation, and other rewards. The behavior of police patrolmen toward their ranking officers provides a number of illustrations of this institutionalized deference: for example, standing at attention while waiting for patrol assignments and using the formal titles, not the first names, of ranking officers. Differences in wearing apparel are often associated with differential prestige. For the rank-and-file police officer, the uniform, complete with ranking insignia, establishes immediate identity and supports his authority.

> Certain symbols . . . tend to become intimately associated with the possession and exercise of authority—crown, throne, and scepter—and often possession of the symbol is itself sufficient to induce respect and authority.[6]

Another characteristic distinguishing hierarchical rank is that superiors generally receive higher compensation. They also have greater access to and control over such valued resources as larger

---

[5] Miller, *op. cit.*, p. 275.

[6] Lasswell and Kaplan, *op. cit.*, p. 136. See also Charles E. Merriam's discussion of the "credenda" (things to be believed) and "miranda" (things to be admired) of authority and power. *Op. cit.*, chap. iv.

offices, newer and better equipment, and freedom to come and go as they please on the job.

This study of authority relations has concentrated on relationships between employees, the incumbents of hierarchical offices in the organization. According to the traditional literature of administration, authority was invested in these positions. The position was, as Leonard D. White maintained, "the universal building block of all organizations."[7] Furthermore, it was authority which defined which of the two positions would be the superior, which the subordinate. The top executive, who received his authority from the governing board, delegated his authority to his subordinates, who, in turn, delegated authority down the "chain of command" until the lowest worker in the hierarchy carried out the routine activities of the organization. These authority relations were institutionalized, that is, they were characterized by explicit rules, predictable behavior, and continuity of relationships. Incumbents might come and go, but authority of position remained.

As has been suggested, it is actually a misconception to speak of the locus of authority, be it position or person, except perhaps for shorthand purposes. Although earlier treatments of authority seem to restrict analysis to formal positions alone, the personal behavior of the incumbents of these positions obviously has considerable impact on the formal structure as it, in turn, conditions their own behavior. However, the study of authority has as its primary focus this series of superior-subordinate relations in organizations. By definition it is less concerned with individual differences than with role relationships. Unlike the traditional administrative theories, however, it does not disregard informal communication channels, friendship cliques, and bases of authority beyond formal position. An additional problem confronting researchers is how far to extend the boundaries of the organization that is being observed. This analysis, like most discussions of bureaucratic authority, has focused on internal authority relations—those taking place between superior and subordinate employees of the organization—rather than external

---

[7] *Introduction to the Study of Public Administration* (4th ed.; New York: Macmillan Co., 1955), p. 40 .

authority relations—those taking place between officials and clientele. In sum, those who are satisfied with the traditional notion of authority may be criticized both for confining analysis to formal membership, thus obscuring distinctions between internal and external authority relationships; and for treating authority as if it were invested solely in formal position, thus neglecting to study the ways in which individual incumbents shape and perceive authority.

Several *temporal* dimensions of authority relations also deserve comment. First, very little empirical work has focused on the importance of formal authority as related to organizational change or stages of growth. As organizations grow more complex and hierarchical levels are added, the importance of authority of position increases. Formal channels of communication replace face-to-face contact; routine operating procedures replace less standard methods of task performance. Top management is increasingly confronted with the need for centralized control and the necessity of decentralized operations.

Second, even less is known about an area in which the temporal dimension merges into environment, namely, the relative importance of formal authority in times of crisis as compared with stable environments and routine behavior. Informal observation of the three organizations which provided the field setting for this study of authority relations suggests that in periods of crisis formal authority is magnified. In situations of minimal or normal conflict, the district director of the welfare office, the police chief, and the elementary school principal did not exercise effective authority merely because of the positions they held. In times of crisis, however, decisions were no longer made at the lowest levels in the hierarchy, but were "bucked upstairs." There appears to be, however, a limit on the importance of position alone. As some of the conclusions of the *American Soldier* studies suggest, it seems to be reached under the impact of strong emotional experiences, such as those shared by officers and enlisted men under combat conditions. The responses of officers, compared with enlisted men, to the importance of formal authority and coercive sanctions as combat motivations revealed striking discrepancies. Officers cited the importance of authority and sanctions more frequently than any other combat incentive, but hardly any of the enlisted men responded in like manner.[8] Not only do these discrepancies support earlier distinctions between the ways in which superiors and subordinates view authority, but they also suggest the hypothesis that, while authority of position may at first increase in importance as the intensity and duration of the shared experience increase, authority of position decreases.

A final temporal phase of authority relationships which needs comment is the distinction between (1) a momentary issuance of a proposal for action by one person and its acceptance by another person as authoritative and (2) role expectations regarding the authority relationship over extended periods—expectations which involve anticipation of obedience on the part of the superior and a willingness to obey on the part of the subordinate.[9] Authority relations are associated with continuing and recurring organizational activities. Tenure by the incumbents of the respective role positions —sergeant and patrolman, supervisor and worker, principal and teacher—extends through time. Although continued acceptance of this role leads to passivity, one rejection is likely to lead to another or to encourage others to evade orders, hence the superior's need to resort to sanctions, even transferring or firing those who are insubordinate, when other bases of authority fail. In general, however, the superior can depend on his employees' bringing with them to the organization certain expectations about the acceptance of formal authority, namely, normative expectations epitomized by the concept of legitimacy.

Authority in and of itself is neither good nor bad; the exercise of authority is not necessarily democratic or undemocratic. Authority becomes good or bad only in particular situations and on the basis of our normative judgments as to the consequences of its exercise. Furthermore, although formal democratic processes may be an important element in the maintenance of authority and organizational cohesion, in other circumstances the same processes may be disruptive and probably are never in themselves sufficient.[10] It is extremely

---

[8] Smith, in Stouffer *et al.*, *op. cit.*, II, 108–112.

[9] Simon, *Administrative Behavior, op. cit.*, p. 126.

[10] Barnard, *The Functions* . . . , *op. cit.*, pp. 167–168, n. 4.

doubtful that what is needed in bureaucratic organizations is, as Bertrand Russell would urge, "local small-scale democracy in all internal affairs" with foremen and managers "elected by those over whom they are to have authority."[11] There is no particular reason that we should expect the techniques of political democracy to be applicable to large-scale bureaucracies, and there are a number of reasons that they probably would not work, among them the necessity for immediate decisions and approximate unanimity of will.

But, as these pronouncements intimate, it is difficult to use the term "authority" in a neutral, descriptive sense. Aside from the ambiguity of the phenomenon itself, this is perhaps the greatest limitation in the possible evolution of the term from a word in everyday use to a more precise, abstract, scientific concept. For, on the one hand, the word is easily transformed into a pejorative adjective, "authoritarian," which is linked with totalitarian forms of rule or objectionable personality syndromes; and, on the other hand, authority implies a notion of "legitimacy," the ethical prescription that individuals ought to obey. The limitations of formal authority should be noted, however.

Authority based on legitimacy and formal position, although basic to the maintenance of organizations, is generally most effective when it is allowed to remain dormant and the sanctions available to the superior remain implicit rather than overt. As Barnard points out:

> Excepting in emergencies and for the settling of disputes or controversies where decision is somewhat of a judicial character, experienced and effective administrators prefer generally not to use authority. Perhaps the most important reason for this reluctance is that to get things done by command relieves the subordinate of responsibility and restricts intelligent freedom of action.[12]

Barnard here refers primarily to formal authority. If the superior can make use of functional authority instead, he is more likely to gain the voluntary support of subordinates. What is more important, subordinates will be more likely to exercise initiative and be more

[11] Bertrand Russell, *Authority and the Individual* (Boston: Beacon Press, 1960), p. 50.
[12] Barnard, review, *op. cit.*, p. 1002.

willing to assume multiple responsibilities.[13] Increased activity and responsibility on the part of subordinates should, in turn, free superiors for more innovative and long-range policy-making.

Although there is a growing body of evidence that increased authority and influence at all levels of the organization are related to increased organizational effectiveness, such an increase in productivity is not without its costs.[14] Greater involvement in and identification with an organization may result in greater conformity at all levels. An increased commitment to the goals of the organization may result in greater personal frustration and anxiety when the goals of the organization are thwarted. These dilemmas appear to be endemic to organizational life. Our knowledge of the consequences of more substantial interaction-influence systems, of increases in the total amount of control, of increased authority exercised by both subordinates and superiors, is still rudimentary.[15] Most of the research on these phenomena has taken place in industry. More studies are needed in governmental bureaucracies.

One aspect of the problem of authority which has been stressed in this study is its impact on the individuals who occupy superior and subordinate positions in organizations. This network of hierarchical positions may also be viewed impersonally in terms of its consequences for the achievement of organizational goals. The authority structure facilitates decision-making, communication, and control, but not without offsetting consequences. The authority structure makes possible specialization in decision-making with the hope that highly rational and effective decisions will be forthcoming. However, conflicts between experts, between subdivisions, and between subunits and more complex divisions are inevitable. The maintenance of social distance between incumbents of positions of authority makes it more likely that impersonal criteria of effective-

---

[13] "Important as formal authority is for meeting the minimum requirements of operations in a complex organization, it is not sufficient for attaining efficiency. It promotes compliance with directives and discipline, but does not encourage employees to exert effort, to accept responsibilities, or to exercise initiative." Blau and Scott, *Formal Organizations, op. cit.,* p. 140.

[14] Arnold S. Tannenbaum, "Control in Organizations: Individual Adjustment and Organizational Performance," *Administrative Science Quarterly,* VII (1962), 236–257.

[15] Likert, *op. cit.*

ness will be used in mediating disputes and making strategic decisions about organizational purposes and means. For the most part, clearly perceived channels of authority expedite the flow of communication. However, differences in status may inhibit the kinds of information that flow along these channels. Superiors may come to hear only what their most immediate subordinates want them to hear. Information from below tends to be discounted for the very reason that it comes from a subordinate. Delegation of authority is one thing; getting people to assume authority once it has been delegated is an even greater problem. When authority fails, sanctions must be invoked even though authority is weakened by frequent resort to sanctions or threats of their use. The executive must continually face and attempt to reconcile these enduring paradoxes. Although the particular type of authority may vary from organization to organization, some form of authority is a functional imperative for the maintenance of the system. When all forms of authority are no longer accepted, formal organizations cease to exist.

APPENDIX

Interview Schedule:
Organizational Relationships

Code
number _____   Date _____
Sex: M _____   Position _____
     F _____   Number of years in position _____
Age   _____   Organization _____
Educ. _____   Number of years with organization _____
Remarks_____   Previous experience _____

First, I want to ask you some questions about (name of organization) as a whole.

1. In your opinion, what are the two or three most important things that (name of organization) should be doing?

    1a) Which of these things do you think is the most important?
    1b) Why?

2. In your opinion, how successful has (name of organization) been in accomplishing these organizational purposes?

143

2a) What leads you to think that?

2b) In the final analysis, would you say that (name of organization), as compared with similar organizations in this area, has been

_____ very successful?

_____ fairly successful?

_____ about average?

_____ fairly unsuccessful?

_____ very unsuccessful?

Now, I would like to ask you a couple of questions about your job.

3. Of all the things you do on your job, what do you consider to be the two or three most important tasks which you perform?

3a) Which of these do you feel is the most important?

3b) Why is that?

4. How does this job stack up as far as personal satisfaction or dissatisfaction?

4a) In particular, what is it about your job which makes you personally satisfied with it?

4b) What is it about your job which makes you personally dissatisfied with it?

4c) In the final analysis, how does this all balance out? Again, on a five-point scale, from one to five, would you say you were

_____ very well satisfied?

_____ fairly well satisfied?

_____ neither satisfied nor dissatisfied?

_____ fairly dissatisfied?

_____ very dissatisfied?

5. In the study of organizations one hears a lot about "authority" and "responsibility." Now these are pretty broad terms, but I'm interested in trying to pin down the meaning of some of these words. What is your definition of these words? What does authority mean to you?

5a) In comparison with other positions in (name of organization), would you say you had

_____ a great deal of authority?
_____ somewhat above average authority?
_____ an average amount of authority?
_____ somewhat below average authority?
_____ no authority at all?

5b) What leads you to say that?

6. People in organizations also talk a lot about "responsibility." What does responsibility mean to you?

6a) To whom are you responsible?
6b) More specifically, probably there are several people in this organization to whom you are responsible. Who are these people? (names and titles)

7. Do you ever get instruction from above which seems to conflict with what you as a (job title) feel you should do? ___ Yes ___ No

7a) (If yes) Can you give me an example? (If no) If you did get such instructions, what would you do?
7b) What do you do then?
7c) How does this work out?

8. Has your superior ever exercised his or her authority in a manner unacceptable to you? _____ Yes _____ No

8a) (If yes) Can you give me an illustration of this? (If no) If he or she had, what would you do?
8b) What did you do about it?
8c) How did this work out?

9. If you and someone else with your same rank have a disagreement, what do you do about it?

9a) If that doesn't work, then what do you do?
9b) In particular, to whom do you go to get the matter settled?
9c) How does that work out?

(If respondent has no subordinates, proceed to Question 12.)

10. What are your responsibilities for supervising the work of others in (name of organization)?

> 10a) How many subordinates report directly to you? _____
> 10b) How many people are you responsible for altogether? _____
>
> 10c) What kinds of people do you supervise?
>
> > _____ professional
> > _____ clerical
> > _____ others

11. How do you go about seeing that your people carry out their jobs?

> 11a) If these things don't work, what do you do then?
> 11b) What do you do if they still refuse to carry out their jobs?

12. Most organizations have some general rules or regulations which the employees are expected to obey. In your opinion, which of these rules and regulations are the most important ones for (name of organization)?

> 12a) Are they always obeyed?
> 12b) What happens when they are disobeyed?

Now I would like to return to your job for a moment.

13. What special skills or training are required for this job?

14. When you need some professional advice or assistance, where do you get it?

> 14a) In particular, what persons do you go to?
> 14b) Why do you go to him (her, them)?
> 14c) If he (she, they) doesn't have the answer, then whom do you go to?

15. Do you belong to any professional organizations or associations? _____ Yes _____ No

15a) (If yes) Which ones?

16. What qualities or personal traits make for a good leader in (name of organization)?

17. More specifically, who do you think is a good leader in (name of organization)?

18. Who really has the final word around here?

Selected Bibliography

The items in this bibliography have been selected because of their importance to the study of authority relations in organizations. It would be of little use to repeat here a number of the titles of less direct relevance which are cited in the body of the book. For a comprehensive bibliography on organizations, containing over eight hundred items classified by type of study, type of organization, and major subject matter (including the topic of supervision, authority relationships, and leadership), see Peter M. Blau and W. Richard Scott, *Formal Organizations* (San Francisco: Chandler Publishing Co., 1962), pp. 258–301.

BOOKS AND MONOGRAPHS

Adorno, T. W., Frenkel-Brunswik, Else, Levinson, Daniel J., and Sanford, R. Nevitt. *The Authoritarian Personality.* New York: Harper & Bros., 1950.

Arensberg, Conrad M., Barkin, Solomon, Chalmers, W. Ellison, Wilensky, Harold L., Worthy, James C., and Dennis, Barbara D. (eds.). *Research in Industrial Human Relations: A Critical Appraisal.* New York: Harper & Bros., 1957.

Argyris, Chris. *Executive Leadership.* New York: Harper & Bros., 1953.
———. *Personality and Organization.* New York: Harper & Bros., 1957.
———. *Understanding Organizational Behavior.* Homewood, Ill.: Dorsey Press, 1960.

Barnard, Chester I. *The Functions of the Executive.* Cambridge: Harvard University Press, 1938.

Baum, Bernard H. *Decentralization of Authority in a Bureaucracy.* Englewood Cliffs, N.J.: Prentice-Hall, Inc., 1961.

Becker, Howard S. "The Teacher in the Authority System of the Public School," in *Complex Organizations,* ed. Amitai Etzioni. New York: Holt, Rinehart, & Winston, 1961.

Bendix, Reinhard. *Work and Authority in Industry.* New York: John Wiley & Sons, 1956.

Benne, Kenneth D. *A Conception of Authority.* New York: Teachers College, Columbia University, 1943.

Bierstedt, Robert K. "The Problem of Authority," in *Freedom and Control in Modern Society,* ed. Morroe Berger, Theodore Abel, and Charles H. Page. New York: Van Nostrand & Co., 1954.

Blau, Peter M. *Bureaucracy in Modern Society.* New York: Random House, 1956.

———. *The Dynamics of Bureaucracy.* Chicago: University of Chicago Press, 1955.

———, and Scott, W. Richard. *Formal Organizations.* San Francisco: Chandler Publishing Co., 1962.

Cartwright, Dorwin (ed.). *Studies in Social Power.* Ann Arbor: Institute for Social Research, 1959.

Comrey, Andrew L., Pfiffner, John M., and High, Wallace S. *Factors Influencing Organizational Effectiveness.* (Office of Naval Research Report.) Los Angeles: University of Southern California, 1954.

Dalton, Melville. *Men Who Manage.* New York: John Wiley & Sons, 1959.

Etzioni, Amitai. *A Comparative Analysis of Complex Organizations.* New York: Free Press of Glencoe, 1961.

Fayol, Henri. *General and Industrial Management.* Translated by Constance Storrs. London: Pitman & Sons, 1949.

Friedrich, Carl J. (ed.). *Authority.* Cambridge: Harvard University Press, 1958.

Gibb, Cecil A. "Leadership," in *Handbook of Social Psychology,* ed. Gardner Lindzey. 2 vols. Reading, Mass.: Addison-Wesley, 1954.

Golembiewski, Robert T. *The Small Group.* Chicago: University of Chicago Press, 1962.

Gouldner, Alvin W. "Organizational Analysis," in *Sociology Today,* ed. Robert K. Merton, Leonard Broom, and Leonard S. Cottrell, Jr. New York: Basic Books, 1959.

————. *The Patterns of Industrial Bureaucracy.* Glencoe, Ill.: Free Press, 1954.

Gulick, Luther H., and Urwick, Lyndall F. (eds.). *Papers on the Science of Administration.* New York: Institute of Public Administration, 1937.

Haire, Mason (ed.). *Modern Organization Theory.* New York: John Wiley & Sons, 1959.

Hartmann, Heinz. *Authority and Organization in German Management.* Princeton: Princeton University Press, 1959.

Hempel, Carl G. "Fundamentals of Concept Formation in Empirical Science," *International Encyclopedia of Unified Science* (1952), II, No. 7.

Homans, George C. *The Human Group.* New York: Harcourt, Brace & Co., 1950.

Hopkins, Terence K. "Bureaucratic Authority: The Convergence of Weber and Barnard," in *Complex Organizations,* ed. Amitai Etzioni. New York: Holt, Rinehart & Winston, 1961.

Jaques, Elliot. *The Changing Culture of a Factory.* London: Tavistock Publications, 1951.

————. *The Measurement of Responsibility.* Cambridge: Harvard University Press, 1956.

Lasswell, Harold D., and Kaplan, Abraham. *Power and Society.* New Haven: Yale University Press, 1950.

Lazarsfeld, Paul F., and Rosenberg, Morris (eds.). *The Language of Social Research.* Glencoe, Ill.: Free Press, 1955.

Leavitt, Harold J. *Managerial Psychology.* Chicago: University of Chicago Press, 1958.

Likert, Rensis. *New Patterns of Management.* New York: McGraw-Hill, 1961.

March, James G., and Simon, Herbert A. *Organizations.* New York: John Wiley & Sons, 1958.

McCleery, Richard. "Communication Patterns as Bases of Systems of Authority and Power," in *Theoretical Studies in Social Organization of the Prison.* New York: Social Science Research Council, 1960.

McGregor, Douglas. *The Human Side of Enterprise.* New York: McGraw-Hill, 1960.

Merton, Robert K., Gray, Ailsa P., Hockey, Barbara, and Selvin, Hanan C. (eds.). *Reader in Bureaucracy.* Glencoe, Ill.: Free Press, 1952.

Michels, Roberto. "Authority," *Encyclopedia of the Social Sciences* (1930), II, 319–321.

Parsons, Talcott. "The Institutionalization of Authority," in Max Weber, *The Theory of Social and Economic Organization.* Translated by A. M. Henderson and Talcott Parsons; ed. Talcott Parsons. New York: Oxford University Press, 1947.

Presthus, Robert. *The Organizational Society.* New York: Alfred A. Knopf, 1962.

Selznick, Phillip. *Leadership in Administration.* Evanston, Ill.: Row, Peterson & Co., 1957.

Simon, Herbert A. *Administrative Behavior* (2nd ed.). New York: Macmillan Co., 1957.

———. *Models of Man.* New York: John Wiley & Sons, 1957.

———, Smithburg, Donald W., and Thompson, Victor A. *Public Administration.* New York: Alfred A. Knopf, 1950.

Simon, Yves. *The Nature and Function of Authority.* Milwaukee: Marquette University Press, 1940.

Stogdill, Ralph M. *Individual Behavior and Group Achievement.* New York: Oxford University Press, 1959.

Thibaut, John W., and Kelley, Harold H. *The Social Psychology of Groups.* New York: John Wiley & Sons, 1959.

Thompson, James D., Hammond, Peter B., Hawkes, Robert W., Junker, Buford H., and Tuden, Arthur (eds.). *Comparative Studies in Administration.* Pittsburgh: University of Pittsburgh Press, 1959.

Thompson, Victor A. *Modern Organization.* New York: Alfred A. Knopf, 1961.

Urwick, Lyndall F. *The Elements of Administration.* New York: Harper & Bros., 1944.

Waldo, Dwight. *The Administrative State.* New York: Ronald Press, 1948.

Weber, Max. *From Max Weber: Essays in Sociology,* ed. H. H. Gerth and C. Wright Mills. New York: Oxford University Press, 1958.

———. *The Theory of Social and Economic Organization.* Translated by A. M. Henderson and Talcott Parsons; ed. Talcott Parsons. New York: Oxford University Press, 1947.

Weiss, Robert S. *Processes of Organization.* Ann Arbor: Institute for Social Research, 1956.

Wolpert, Jeremiah. "Toward a Sociology of Authority," in *Studies in Leadership,* ed. Alvin W. Gouldner. New York: Harper & Bros., 1950.

ARTICLES AND PERIODICALS

Adams, J. S., and Romney, A. K. "A Functional Analysis of Authority," *Psychological Review,* LXVI (1959), 234–251.

"Authority," *International Social Science Bulletin,* VII (1955), 665–668.

Banfield, Edward C., review of Herbert A. Simon's *Administrative Behavior* (2nd ed.), in *Public Administration Review,* XVII (1957), 278–285.

Barnard, Chester I., review of Charles S. Hyneman's *Bureaucracy in a Democracy,* in *American Political Science Review,* XLIV (1950), 990–1004.

Bates, F. L., and White, Rodney F. "Differential Perceptions of Authority in Hospitals," *Journal of Health and Human Behavior,* II (1961), 262–267.

Bennis, Warren G. "Leadership Theory and Administrative Behavior: The Problem of Authority," *Administrative Science Quarterly,* IV (1959), 259–301.

———, Berkowitz, N., Affinito, M., and Malone, M. "Authority, Power and the Ability to Influence," *Human Relations,* XI (1958), 143–155.

Blau, Peter M. "Critical Remarks on Weber's Theory of Authority," *American Political Science Review,* LVII (1963), 305–316.

Browne, Clarence G. "Study of Executive Leadership in Business. I. The R, A, and D Scales," *Journal of Applied Psychology,* XXXIII (1949), 521–526.

Campbell, Donald T., and McCormack, T. H. "Military Experience and Attitudes Toward Authority," *American Journal of Sociology,* LXII (1957), 482–490.

Coates, C. H., and Pellegrin, R. J. "Executives and Supervisors: Contrasting Self-conceptions and Conceptions of Each Other," *American Sociological Review,* XXII (1957), 217–220.

Coleman, James S. "Relational Analysis: The Study of Social Organizations with Survey Methods," *Human Organization,* XVII (1958–1959), 28–36.

Coser, Rose Laub. "Authority and Decision-Making in a Hospital: A Comparative Analysis," *American Sociological Review,* XXIII (1958), 56–63.

Dahl, Robert A. "The Concept of Power," *Behavioral Science,* II (1957), 201–215.

Duffy, Daniel J. "Authority Considered from an Operational Point of View," *Journal of the Academy of Management,* II (1959), 167–175.

Emerson, Richard M. "Power-Dependency Relations," *American Sociological Review,* XXVII (1962), 31–41.

Evan, William M., and Zelditch, Morris, Jr. "Experiment on Bureaucratic Authority," *American Sociological Review,* XX (1961), 883–893.

Etzioni, Amitai. "Authority Structure and Organizational Effectiveness," *Administrative Science Quarterly,* IV (1959), 43–67.

Feld, M. D. "Information, Authority, and Military Organization," *American Sociological Review,* XXIV (1959), 15–22.

Follett, Mary Parker. "The Illusion of Final Authority," *Bulletin of the Taylor Society,* XI (1926), 243–246. Reprinted in part in Albert Lewpawsky (ed.). *Administration.* New York: Alfred A. Knopf, 1955.

Friedrich, Carl J. "Political Leadership and the Problem of Charismatic Power," *Journal of Politics,* XXIII (1961), 3–24.

Gibbon, I. G. "The Official and His Authority," *Public Administration,* IV (1926), 81–94.

Golembiewski, Robert T. "The Small Group and Public Administration," *Public Administration Review,* XIX (1959), 149–156.

———. "Some Notes on Presthus' 'Authority in Organizations,' " *Public Administration Review,* XXI (1961), 171–175.

Grazia, Sebastian de. "What Authority Is *Not,*" *American Political Science Review,* LIII (1959), 321–331.

Harrison, Paul M. "Weber's Categories of Authority and Voluntary Associations," *American Sociological Review,* XXV (1960), 232–237.

James, H. Thomas. "The Nature of Professional Authority," *Phi Delta Kappan,* XLI (1959), 45–48.

Janowitz, Morris. "Changing Patterns of Organizational Authority: The Military Establishment," *Administrative Science Quarterly,* III (1959), 473–493.

Mandeville, Merten J. "The Nature of Authority," *Journal of the Academy of Management,* III (1960), 107–118.

McMurry, Robert N. "The Case for Benevolent Autocracy," *Harvard Business Review,* XXXVI (1958), 82–90.

Miller, Walter B. "Two Concepts of Authority," *American Anthropologist,* LVII (1955), 271–289.

Morse, Nancy C., Reimer, Everett, and Tannenbaum, Arnold S. "Regulation and Control in Hierarchical Organizations," *Journal of Social Issues,* VII (1951), 41–48.

Porter, L. W. "Differential Self-Perceptions of Management Personnel and Line Workers," *Journal of Applied Psychology,* XLII (1958), 105–109.

Presthus, Robert V. "Toward a Theory of Organizational Behavior," *Administrative Science Quarterly,* III (1958), 48–72.

———. "Authority in Organizations," *Public Administration Review,* XX (1960), 86–91.

Richardson, Stephen A. "Organizational Contrasts on British and American Ships," *Administrative Science Quarterly,* I (1956), 189–207.

Schutz, Alfred. "Concept and Theory Formation in the Social Sciences," *Journal of Philosophy,* LI (1954), 257–273.

Simon, Herbert A. " 'The Decision-Making Schema': A Reply," *Public Administration Review,* XVIII (1958), 60–63.

Simpson, Richard L. "Vertical and Horizontal Communication in Formal Organizations," *Administrative Science Quarterly,* IV (1959), 188–196.

Stagner, R. "Attitude toward authority: an exploratory study," *Journal of Social Psychology,* XL (1954), 197–210.

Stein, Ludwig. "The Sociology of Authority," *Papers and Proceedings of the American Sociological Society,* XVIII (1923), 116–120.

Suojanen, Waino W. "Leadership, Authority, and the Span of Control," *Advanced Management,* XXII (1957), 17–22.

Sykes, Gresham M. "The Corruption of Authority and Rehabilitation," *Social Forces,* XXXIV (1956), 257–262.

———. "The Structure of Authority," *Public Opinion Quarterly,* XVII (1953), 146–150.

Tannenbaum, Arnold S. "The Concept of Organization Control," *Journal of Social Issues,* XII (1956), 50–60.

———. "Control in Organizations: Individual Adjustment and Organizational Performance," *Administrative Science Quarterly,* VII (1962), 236–257.

Tannenbaum, Robert. "Managerial Decision-Making," *Journal of Business,* XXIII (1950), 22–39.

Thompson, James D. "Authority and Power in 'Identical' Organizations," *American Journal of Sociology,* LXII (1956), 290–301.

Udy, Stanley H., Jr. "The Structure of Authority in Non-industrial Production Organizations," *American Journal of Sociology,* LXIV (1959), 582–584.

Whisler, Thomas L. "The 'Assistant-to' in Four Administrative Settings," *Administrative Science Quarterly,* V (1960), 182–216.

Zalkind, Sheldon S., and Costello, Timothy W. "Perception: Some Recent Research and Implications for Administration," *Administrative Science Quarterly,* VII (1962), 218–235.

Index

157